W9-BIY-925

Bringing
Your
Teen
Back
to
God

H 11373 20.00

Lamppost Library & Resource Center
Christ United Methodist Church
Poplar Avenue
Memphis Tennessee 38117

LIFEJOURNEY
BOOKS

David C. Cook Publishing Co.

Elgin, Illinois • Weston, Ontario
Nova Distribution Ltd., Torquay, England

LifeJourney Books is an imprint of David C. Cook Publishing Co.
David C. Cook Publishing Co., Elgin, Illinois 60120
David C. Cook Publishing Co., Weston, Ontario
Nova Distribution, Ltd., Torquay, England

Cover design by Matt Key
Interior design by Dawn Lauck

BRINGING YOUR TEEN BACK TO GOD
Copyright ©1991 by Bob Laurent

All rights reserved. Except for brief excerpts for review purposes, no part of this book may be reproduced or used in any form without written permission from the publisher.

First Printing, 1991
Printed in the United States of America
95 94 93 92 91 5 4 3 2 1

Library of Congress Cataloging in Publication Data
Laurent, Bob.
Bringing your teen back to God/Bob Laurent.
p. cm.
Includes bibliographical reference and index.
ISBN 1-55513-317-7
1. Teenagers—Religious life. 2. Parenting—Religious aspects—Christianity.
I. Title.
BV4531.2L385   1991
248.8'45—dc20   91-26443
                                                 CIP

TABLE OF CONTENTS

DEDICATED TO

My hero, Carl William Laurent, Jr.; a husband whose best friend is his wife; a teacher whose favorite subject is his God; and a father whose highest prayer is for his children to know the lordship of Jesus Christ and to follow him into the joys of heaven.

FOREWORD

Bob Laurent's ability to communicate with young people is his gift. His godly family is a living testimony to the effectiveness of that gift.

I have known Bob for many years and have continued to be amazed at his insight and wisdom. His understanding of teens draws them to him. It drew me as a teen, and it changed my life forever. Bob's sense of humor, his caring spirit, and his ability to communicate Christ has impacted countless thousands of young people.

While many people have influenced the style of music that I play—Bob Laurent influenced the content.

MICHAEL W. SMITH

PREFACE

More than 85 percent of those who decide for Christ do so before the age of nineteen. If our children do not embrace the Christian faith during their teen years, the prospects of them becoming Christians later are, statistically speaking, dismal at best. Of course there is always hope, but the following story is becoming too common.

Diane grew up in a prominent Christian home in central Illinois. Deeply loved by parents who were actively involved in her church's youth program, Diane couldn't remember a time when her life was not neatly defined by the protective borders of Christianity. Until her sophomore year in high school, she sang in the youth choir, attended most church functions voluntarily, and even participated in a summer mission project to an Indian reservation in New Mexico. She was, in many respects, the model Christian daughter.

Along with her middle teenage years, however, came a growing coolness toward the church. As she began to pull away from her Christian friends and hang out with the more "popular" kids at school, it became a constant battle to get her to attend any youth group meetings. Her mood swings became meteoric, and her disdain for being at home obvious.

During her junior year, Diane's parents suspected that she had been drinking and privately worried that she was no longer a virgin. Their attempts to talk to her about their suspicions inevitably erupted into ugly confrontations. Once open and warm, their relationship with their daughter, who was daily becoming more of a stranger to them, was now marked by tension and mutual silence.

Whenever she came home from being with her non-Christian boyfriend, she usually went right to her room, locked the door, turned up her stereo and commandeered the telephone for the remainder of the evening. Frustrated and perplexed by her behavior, her parents began to pray together each morning for her return to the faith of her childhood. Emotionally exhausted from fighting with her, they resigned themselves just to getting her through these difficult years with the least amount of damage.

But in mid-July of the summer before her senior year in high school, a slippery road at midnight and a 19-year-old driver under the influence of alcohol ended any chance that Diane's parents had to get her through her teenage years. Weeks after the funeral, her father sought me out for counsel. His languid eyes, swollen from crying, betrayed the sleepless nights that had become a ritual for him.

Ten minutes into our conversation about the guilt he and his wife were struggling with, he stared blankly at the filing cabinet beside me and said, "It's not enough, you know." Sensing that he was changing the subject, I asked, "What's not enough, Phil?" He shifted his vacuous gaze to the Bible on my desk and replied, "It's just not enough that they grow up in a Christian home, and attend church every Sunday, and go to Vacation Bible School from the time they're little kids." He looked up at me and said with emotion, "Something has to happen to them when they become teenagers, doesn't it?" It was more of a statement than a question, a truth that he and his wife had learned the hard way.

Even before this tragedy, I had begun to research the problem of teenagers leaving the church. The findings of that study are in my first book, *Keeping Your Teen in Touch With God*. After Diane's death, however, I determined to discover the most effective ways to evangelize today's teenagers. It is perhaps more difficult to "get" them in touch with God than to keep them there.

I was already convinced of what Diane's father had just realized—that what happens spiritually during adolescence will literally change a teen's life forever. What a person decides about Jesus Christ *during his teenage years* is crucial. This decision is not only a prelude to the eventual shape of his religious belief; it is often a reliable indicator of how well a teen will handle the enormous pressures of adolescence.

The results of my two year study of 1,200 youths nationwide reveal important principles for evangelizing modern teenagers. There are answers to the urgent question, "How can I help my teen decide for Christ?" One of the most helpful aspects of this book is that many of those answers come from our teens themselves. You will be challenged by their honesty, encouraged by their insights, and surprised by many of their responses.

Where can parents and youth pastors go for help in reaching their teenagers with God's love? There is very little Christian literature available that is based on empirical research dealing with this vital topic. This book is, in part, an answer to that need.

Serving you,
serving Him,

BOB LAURENT

CHAPTER
1

If You Could Do
It Over Again . . .

"A man should never be ashamed to own he has been in the wrong, which is but saying he is wiser today than he was yesterday."— ALEXANDER POPE

TEENAGERS! JUST WHEN YOU think you've got them figured out, they put gas in the family car or set the dinner table without being asked.

What is a teenager? Answer that question and you are light years ahead of most adolescent psychologists, who are still debating the "nature versus nurture" controversy. Were my children "born to be wild," or is it my parenting style that's driving them to be teenage terrorists?

It's a moot point. I'm not really concerned about the fountain of genes that has produced my teens; it's that mountain of jeans on their bedroom floor that bothers me. What is a teenager? Don't be confused by the behavioral scientists. Ask any parent. A teenager is:

- a volatile bundle of lethal hormones—ready to explode at the least provocation.
- a hopeless romantic who can be counted on not to fall in love . . . more than twice a week.
- a Rambo-in-training who lifts weights for two hours every night, never misses a chance to catch a pass, steal a base, or make a lay-up—and has to be driven to the garbage can.
- a computer genius who can conquer the latest Nintendo

game without reading the manual, but can't learn how to make a bed.

- a budding beauty who spends twice as long in front of the mirror as she does on her homework—proving that she has learned that boys can see better than they can think.
- a misunderstood martyr who is convinced that neither of his parents were ever teenagers.

What are teenagers? They're the warmest/least friendly, brightest/most obtuse, easiest understood/most enigmatic people I've ever met. They are an endangered species, *Teenagerus americanus*—endangered because we who brought them into the world are often on the verge of taking them out of it.

TRUE CONFESSIONS FROM PARENTS

Soon after our second child reached thirteen, I saw a pattern emerging. All of our offspring planned on becoming teenagers. I think that's when I started getting paranoid about my parenting skills and began asking parents of seemingly docile teens how they did it.

Their answers were usually vague and not very encouraging: "I guess we're just lucky," or "You don't really know our kids; they aren't perfect. Why, both of them got a B on their last report card."

Then I realized that I was asking the wrong question. Drawing on years of parenting by trial and error, I changed my question to this: "If you had to raise your teens over again, what would you have done differently?"

The floodgates opened. These parents were waiting for a listening ear, for the chance to verbalize what had been on their minds for years. Normally taciturn adults sought me out to offer their hard-earned wisdom. I had struck a universal nerve. If Oscar Wilde was right when he observed, "Experience is the name everyone gives to their mistakes," then there is a lot of experience in these confessions from the parents of teens. Here are some of their responses.

I would have taught them the basics of cooking when they were younger and always underfoot in the kitchen. Today they act like I'm sending them to the front lines of a battle, unarmed, if I ask them to make a salad for dinner. —MOTHER OF THREE TEENS

I'd have shown her that I really cared about what she had to say, no matter how long it took her to get it out. Maybe then she would have kept talking to me when she became a teen.

—MOTHER OF A TEENAGE RUNAWAY

The most common piece of advice went something like this:

I'd have spent more time with them. Now that I want to be with them, they don't want to be with me.—DIVORCED FATHER OF TWO TEENS

I'd have taken time for them when they were younger. Even though their bodies are in the house for eighteen years, they're really yours mentally and emotionally only for a short while. Now I feel cheated.

—MOTHER OF TWO TEENS

Had girls.

—MOTHER OF FIVE BOYS, WHOSE HOUSE USUALLY LOOKS LIKE THE SITE OF A DEMOLITION DERBY

Had boys.

—MOTHER OF FOUR GIRLS, WHO CAN'T FIND A CURLING IRON OR A VACANT BATHROOM

I would have gotten them involved in great causes like pro-life and anti-pornography when they were younger, instead of trying to protect them from life's tough realities. Now they think they're being politically active when they vote for Diet Coke over Diet Pepsi.

—CHRISTIAN ACTIVIST AND MOTHER OF THREE TEENS

When we got beyond the humor and nostalgia, most parents expressed a concern about the spiritual status of their teens. The comments which moved me the most had eternal significance.

I would have prioritized what's important much earlier; having an intimate relationship with God and being a caring person is way up there. Keeping their rooms tidy and their hair trimmed is not.

—SCHOOL PRINCIPAL AND MOTHER OF FOUR TEENS

My husband and I should have sat down and worked out our beliefs so we could be united on the big issues like religion, death, and sex. Now my son wants to stay home with his father on Sunday morning while I take the girls to church.—WIFE OF A WEEKEND ARMCHAIR QUARTERBACK

11

I would have led my child to Christ. I became a Christian when my daughter was already a teen. Now she wants nothing to do with church.

—*MOTHER OF A HIGH-SCHOOL CHEERLEADER*

These responses inspired me to poll a hundred Christian parents (fifty mothers, fifty fathers) to find out their greatest fear for their teenagers. Each parent answered the following question.

Please check off the top three fears that you have for your teen(s):

Negative influence from friends   _____
Involvement with drugs   _____
Premarital sex   _____
Not finding a good job after graduation   _____
A broken relationship with you as the parent   _____
Marriage to the wrong person   _____
Lack of commitment to the Christian faith   _____
Premature death   _____
Unfinished education   _____

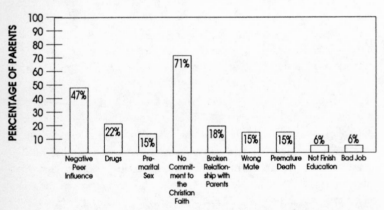

CHART NO. 1: THE GREATEST FEARS OF CHRISTIAN PARENTS

Youth evangelist Rich Wilkerson warns, "1.5 million teens between thirteen and seventeen are alcoholics; 1.8 million kids run away from home every year; there are over ten million single-parent homes, and some one in ten Americans are admitted homosexuals. What a time to raise up kids without God!"[1]

Christian parents are listening. They must. Their fear for their teens' future is compelling them. Jay Kesler notes, "Parents who may be impregnable to almost everything else have this one chink in their armor; they are concerned about teenagers, especially their own."[2]

Wondering how different the fears of non-Christian parents would be, I administered the same survey among a hundred parents (fifty mothers, fifty fathers) from non-Christian homes. The results were what I expected.

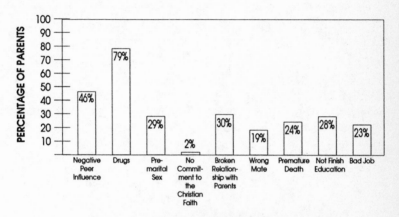

CHART NO. 2: THE GREATEST FEARS OF NON-CHRISTIAN PARENTS

Both Christian (forty-seven percent) and non-Christian parents (forty-six percent) have one major fear in common: they are afraid that their teenagers will mix with the wrong kind of friends (negative peer influence). But the greatest fear of Christian parents hardly registers with parents from unchurched backgrounds: the fear that their teens will decide against Christianity. Again and again, church-related parents registered their anxiety, completing the thought "My greatest fear for my teenager(s) is . . ." with answers like the following.

. . . that they will not choose Christ as Savior and Guide, and allow Him to direct their lives.

. . . that they would not be saved.

. . . that her relationship with Christ and the church will not be strong enough to sustain her when she has to make tough choices that will affect her for the rest of her life.

. . . that he will not stand up for his Christian beliefs.

Perhaps the response that best represents the fear most common to Christian parents came from a mother in Mississippi:

"My greatest fear is that we as parents have not done the best job we can to introduce our teenagers to Christ and prepare them to deal with today's problems."

The good news is that there is much hope for the future faith of our teenagers, and we as parents can play a significant role in their decision to follow Jesus Christ. In fact, if we parents learn how to be "as wise as serpents and as harmless as doves," I believe teens are more reachable today than ever before. It is my highest prayer that this book will:

1. help parents recognize how teenagers become Christians and what can be done to facilitate their decision for Christ.
2. show parents how to translate their fear and guilt into positive steps for leading their teens to Christ.
3. provide key, biblical insights for turning teens toward the Christian faith.
4. enable parents to understand better the adolescent psyche and implement that knowledge to promote their teens' active involvement with Christianity.
5. offer fresh, practical suggestions to improve parent/teen communication.
6. help parents remove the barriers that keep their teens from knowing Jesus Christ.
7. point the way to more loving friendships between parents and their teenagers.

Years ago a wise man advised me that if I wanted to be effective in youth ministry I must work hard to make myself an interpreter— interpreting teens to adults and adults to teens. I have taken that mandate seriously.

But there is another gap to be closed which might be the interpreter's more important and difficult task. It is the distance between who the interpreter's hearers are and who they might become. Whether parent, pastor, or teen, you will see yourself in the pages that follow. Who you become as you read them is up to you . . . and God. I have great hope for you.

CHAPTER
2

The Reasons Teens Become Christians

Discovering Teenage Entry
Levels into the Christian Faith

I LIVE WITH MY FAMILY IN A western suburb of Chicago. Being a Christian with a bit of a persecution complex, it is not difficult for me to root for the Chicago Cubs. I mean, we haven't won the National League pennant since 1945 (when the other teams' players went off to war) or a World Series since 1908 B.C. (Before Curve balls). How much suffering can a sports fan take? Still, hope springs eternal at Wrigley Field.

As interesting as the Chicago sports scene can be, it hardly makes up for the Windy City's unpredictable weather patterns. During one week-long stretch of sub-zero temperatures and windchills as cold as eighty degrees below, I was listening to a weather forecast. The meteorologist said, "Today's weather will again be bright and bitter . . . a lot like today's teenagers."

You don't expect astute sociological observations from your local weatherman, but, of course, he was right. And why shouldn't teenagers be bitter? When today's high school seniors were born, Nixon was denying any knowledge of Watergate. When they entered kindergarten, abortionists were on their way to killing more Americans than were lost in Vietnam. With junior high school came repeated sex scandals among some of America's best known religious and political leaders. Now in high school, at a time when they seek truth and need answers, they are pawns in a curriculum characterized by relativism and New Age philosophies. Why shouldn't they be bitter?

THE FALLOUT OF FOUR DECADES

This bitterness was predictable. Consider what has been lost in our society since World War II. In the 1950s, youth lost their innocence. The moral consensus that had undergirded America for 200 years was crumbling. The sexual rebellion was beginning. In the 1960s, the teen generation lost their authority. Respect for leadership in government, on the home front, and in the church was on the wane. With the 70s (the "decade of me") came the loss of love. As divorce enervated the family and "the pill" dehumanized American high school girls, the teenager's world became a lonely place. Finally, in the logical progression of losses, the enigmatic 80s saw teens lose their hope.[1]

According to the National Center for Health Statistics, the rate of suicide has doubled since 1980, making suicide the second-leading cause of death among teens (after car accidents). Over 100,000 teenagers will attempt suicide this year, while about 250,000 others will seriously consider it.[2] In some communities, suicide has reached epidemic proportions, leaving shattered parents riddled with guilt from lessons learned too late.

"She was a beautiful girl," wrote a grief-stricken mother, telling me of the suicide death of her sixteen-year-old daughter, Sarah. "My heart aches so much when I allow myself to think how wonderful things could have been for Sarah if she had embraced Christianity as I have. She just didn't have the strength, emotional confidence, and loving support of her family to actually believe that she could be loved by God—especially after some of her mistakes. She was convinced she was not worth loving and that it was just too hard to live up to those Christian standards. How so very sad that she never realized that the same God she was rejecting was the only one who could love her totally, including even me. He would have forgiven her anything. He could have set her free from her pain when we, her parents, just didn't have the answers."

ADOLESCENCE: THE "WANDER" YEARS

"High school is the first time a teenager can make mature decisions. Therefore, it is the crucial time to introduce him to Jesus Christ," says Jay Kesler, past president of Youth for Christ. "The problem is that there is a great gap between the death of Christ for them and the modern teenager. It happens to be our privilege (as Christian parents) to stand in the gap, to hold in one hand the hand of the Lord Jesus and in the other the hand of the teenager for whom He died. That's called evangelism."[3] Helping parents to effect such evangelism is what this book is all about.

Sarah's mother was perceptive. She saw the real tragedy behind her daughter's premature death: ". . . the same God she was rejecting was the only one who could . . . set her free." The fallout of the past four decades cannot be dealt with successfully by secular panaceas. After twenty years in youth work, I am convinced that only a personal relationship with Jesus Christ can answer the heart's cry of today's teenager.

For those who have lost their innocence, He offers forgiveness. *"Has no one condemned you? . . . Neither do I." (John 8:10, 11)*

For those who have lost authority, He offers unfailing leadership. *"He will not fail you or forsake you." (I Chronicles 28:20)*

For teens who have suffered the loss of love, He offers unconditional mercy. *"His love endures forever." (Psalm 100:5)*

And youth who have lost hope and face despair will find in Christ a life of true meaning and purpose. *"Happy is the man . . . whose hope is in the Lord." (Psalm 146:5, TLB)*

According to Dann Spader of Sonlife Ministries, eighty-five percent of those who decide for Christ do so before their eighteenth birthday.[4] Comparatively few people make decisions to join the Christian faith after high school, making adolescence the crucial time to lead our teens to Jesus Christ.

Both research and common sense experience have shown me two key factors about teens that serve as primary motivations for my work.

1. Teenagers, ever the seekers for truth, are still wonderfully reachable when they make contact with biblical Christianity.

George Gallup's annual religious surveys among adolescents have had a common theme for years: American teens desire to know God and are still interested in getting spiritual answers to their questions about life. In my own survey, I received hundreds of positive statements from teens regarding their openness to New Testament evangelism.

I'm not a Christian yet, but I wish I were. I only started going to church this year, but I plan on coming for quite a long time.

—HEATHER, *14*

My best friend brought me to camp with her. One night after cabin devotions, our counselor led a prayer and invited us to accept Christ. I did.—GREG, *17*

I was so depressed that I didn't want to live anymore. Then I got invited to go to a youth group meeting at church. Those guys didn't care who I was or what I'd done. They just loved me right from the start. I wanted what they had, and I found it in Jesus.—ANDY, *16*

After I got pregnant and had an abortion, my boyfriend didn't want anything to do with me. I never felt so alone in my life. Then a girl in my P.E. class asked me to go on a Campus Life Breakaway with her to Florida. The speaker was great. It was just like he was talking to me. When he told us how much God loved us and that Jesus died for our sins, I knew this was what I was looking for. My parents don't understand me yet, but they can tell that I'm different from what I used to be.—KIM, *15*

2. *Although still receptive to the Gospel, the fact is that most teenagers remain non-Christians.*

Jay Kesler believes that we parents need "a new understanding of the religious makeup of teenage America." The mere fact that there is much religious interest among adolescents does not signify that there are a large percentage of committed Christians among our teens. Kesler fears that the opposite may be the truth.

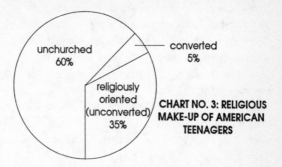

CHART NO. 3: RELIGIOUS MAKE-UP OF AMERICAN TEENAGERS

Kesler claims that only five percent of teenagers can be classified as Christian (or converted). The other ninety-five percent (unconverted) of teenage America consists of religiously oriented teens (thirty-five percent) and unchurched teens (sixty percent).[5] If these statistics are anywhere near being accurate, then evangelism among teens must become a priority for parents and the church.

REACHING THE OTHER NINETY-FIVE

This book is not concerned with the five percent who are obviously committed to the lordship of Jesus Christ. I meet these fresh-faced kids (and many of the same ones over and over again) at large youth conferences all over the country. They are vocal about their faith, highly visible in the church, and energized to share Christ's love with their friends. But they are in a minority among America's teens, even among the religiously oriented teens. My concern is with the ninety-five percent in need of a conversion experience.

I have observed four basic types of unconverted teens.

1. The unchurched teen is the most evident type.

The very numbers of this group exert tremendous influence on its own members, as well as on the religious teen. These teenagers are encouraged by the prevailing mood of our society to "party hearty," and often have no qualms about inviting your church-related teen along for the ride. They seldom have any interest in organized religion and are quick to point out the hypocrisy of the church and any of its members in their acquaintance. I have met these teens in high schools nationwide.

One day, after speaking at a public high school convocation, I engaged a male student in conversation. We were both waiting by the front door of the school for our respective rides.

"My name's Bob. I'm the guy who spoke today at your assembly. What did you think of it?"

"Oh, yeah, it was pretty good," he replied, smiling. "I liked some of your stories. My name is Tony."

After we shook hands, I said, "Thanks a lot. You guys were great to listen like you did. Are you a Christian?" (That's a question I almost always ask if it's natural, because it can open up so many possibilities for discussion.)

"Uh, no. I, uh, don't think so."

I had a fairly good idea of what he thought a Christian was, so I asked, "What do you think about God?"

Until this moment, he was at ease with me; now he seemed confused.

"I don't know what you mean, man."

I decided to get to the point. "Okay, what do you think of Jesus Christ?"

He looked up at me, then glanced out the window and replied, "I really don't know what you mean."

Normally, I would have considered changing the subject until I knew him better, or at least altered my approach. But for some reason, this time I pressed it.

"All right, then, what do you think about the church?"

I'll always admire that young man for the integrity of his response.

"Look, mister," he said, turning toward me and not taking his eyes from mine. "I don't want to offend you, but I don't think about God. I don't think about Jesus Christ, and I sure don't think about the church." He paused for a moment and said, matter-of-factly, "I think about the real world."

It was just as well that a car horn honked for him then, because I had no response. This incident occurred over ten years ago, and I still believe that his answer is a telling example of how most unchurched teens feel about the Christian religion. They want real answers for real problems and have come to associate religion with unreality and impotence—like a useless relic from the past. Organized religion might be meaningful for some adults and the "uncool" fringe of teenage America, but it has nothing to do with the real concerns of their immediate world.

Still, hope must run high for the evangelization of this largest group of non-Christian teens. Bill Bright of Campus Crusade believes that "at least twenty-five percent of non-Christian teens would accept Christ right now if properly approached by a Spirit-filled Christian trained to communicate the Gospel."[6]

The other three types of unconverted teen have a religious orientation, but could hardly be considered committed Christians in the classical biblical sense.

2. The outwardly rebellious teen actively shows signs of disengaging from the church.

Such young people are openly critical of all things religious; the sermons are boring; the other teens in the youth group are either "phony" or simply "nerds." They openly defy their parents' wishes that they attend church functions. Although there was a time when they enjoyed contemporary Christian music, now the Christian station is anathema to them, and the sounds from their bedroom radios are all secular rock.

Their closest friendships are with non-Christian friends from school. Just like the next two types, they exhibit no concern to share their Christian experience with their school friends. In fact, about the only difference between these teens and their non-Christian companions is that they are expected to attend worship service with their parents. They are likely candidates to leave the church. Forty-six percent of Americans withdraw from active religious participation at some point in their lives, the rate of withdrawal being greatest among adolescents.[7]

3. The inwardly rebellious teen characterizes my own experience as a church-related youth.

The Lord Jesus depicted my condition aptly when He quoted the prophet Isaiah: "These people honor me with their lips, but their hearts are far from me" (Matthew 15:8).

Such teenagers realize early what it takes to gain the praise and approval of their parents and other authority figures. Never openly hostile, they are often alienated from and inwardly critical of religion, but wouldn't dare express it for fear of the consequences. Under the watchful eyes of their parents, they will get good grades, never smoke, drink, or carouse openly. But once they are emancipated from parental control, they are likely to throw off the trappings of a religion that always seems to take the joy out of their lives. As a professor at a Christian college, I have seen these students time and again experience their "coming out party" after leaving home, living in open rebellion against the religious standards of their parents.

4. *The apathetic religious teen is just as likely to disengage from the church upon high school graduation.*

These teenagers produce the most anxiety and discouragement in youth pastors and often reduce their ministry to glorified baby-sitting. They are well-described by the apostle Paul as those who "go to church . . . but they won't really believe anything they hear" (II Timothy 3:5, TLB). Marked by self-preoccupation and spiritual indifference, they simply do not care about the mission of the church. They are in a holding pattern, marking their time, doing their religious duty in a mindless fashion. Neither outwardly nor inwardly rebellious in high school, they usually drift along with religion until they make contact with a non-Christian peer group at the university level.

THE NEED FOR AN "INNER CONVERSION"

These last three types of religiously oriented teens have experienced what some theorists call an "outer conversion," described as a formal action of external identification with the Christian faith. "What church-related teenagers need," says psychologist H. N. Malony, "is an 'inner conversion,' referring to a newly acquired sense of inner security, unity, peace, and meaning such as is exemplified in the apostle Paul when he asserts, 'I have been crucified with Christ and I no longer live, but Christ lives in me' (Galatians 2:20)."[8]

Malony contends that often teens' joining of a given church or religious group (termed "outer conversion") is mistaken for a radical change in their perception and outlook (termed "inner conversion").[9] Simply put, an experience of inner conversion means that the teenager has turned away from sin and self while turning toward the saving and keeping power of the Lord Jesus Christ. It is usually critical that this conversion occurs during the adolescent years.

In *Adolescence: Identity and Crisis*, Erik Erikson defines adolescence as a unique period of identity formation during which the teen is remarkably open to a reconsideration of the meaning and purpose of life.[10] It is only logical that most conversions would happen during the period in which teens are struggling for independence and searching for new authority in their lives.

During adolescence, teenagers begin to see both the limits and possibilities of living selfishly. No amount of reason or appeal to conscience can change them from this greedy track. Only the Christian Gospel can open a teenager up to the possibilities of genuine loving. G. Stanley Hall, in his classic *Adolescence*, says that the Gospel is "the most powerful psychological force in converting teenagers from a life of selfishness to the life of love for which God created them."[11]

But the corollary is also true. Adolescence is that time when most teenagers unwittingly choose against Christianity. It is a fact that over fifty percent of Christian teenagers will sit in church next Sunday morning, only to have seventy percent of those leave the church within two years, never to return.[12]

If approximately ninety-five percent of American teenagers are in need of an "inner conversion" (and almost forty percent of those are church-related), then it seemed to me that a study of the reasons that teens become Christians would be a significant project. So much of the literature regarding teens and evangelism is characterized by conjecture and personal opinion that I determined from the beginning that my study would meet the requirements of the scientific method. The results offer empirical evidence on a subject about which I am aware of no other scientific research having been conducted. I also decided that this study would go beyond external observation to probe the innermost feelings of the teens who were surveyed, taking them seriously and honestly attempting to listen to them.

The first step in this project was to identify and isolate specific teenage entry levels into the Christian faith. From years of evangelizing and counseling teens, I recognized certain factors surfacing again and again. I devised a questionnaire in which I included eight recurring themes, and asked Christian teens nationwide to choose those factors which led them to faith in Jesus Christ. I interviewed over 1,200 randomly selected Christian teenagers.

The results of the questionnaire are revealed in this book, with the eight major causes for teenage conversion dealt with in the order that the teens themselves ranked them. Before you read further, it might be interesting for you to rank the eight causes yourself. Score them the way you think teens in the survey did, giving a 1 to the influence that you believe would cause the most teens to come to Christ, a 2 to the second highest cause, and so on.

Reasons That Teenagers Become Christians

	My guess	Teens' ranking
Influence of Satanic Encounter	_____	_____
Having Questions Answered (or Doubts Dealt with)	_____	_____
Influence of Christian Media	_____	_____
Influence of a Crisis (or Suffering)	_____	_____
Influence of Youth Pastor	_____	_____
Influence of Christian Friends	_____	_____
Influence of Church	_____	_____
Parental Influence	_____	_____

As you are about to read, the teenagers interviewed expressed their feelings with refreshing candor and heartfelt emotion. They had some important things to say to us about the reasons they became Christians, and what we can do to help others make that decision. Using the results of this study to help parents and youth pastors influence their teens toward a vibrant faith in Jesus Christ is the major purpose of this book.

(The eight causes are listed above in reverse order of the teens' actual ranking. How did you do?)

CHAPTER
3

The Parent
as Evangelist

By the time a man realizes that maybe his father was
right, he usually has a son who thinks he's wrong.
—CHARLES WADSWORTH

Lamppost Library & Resource Center
Christ United Methodist Church
4488 Poplar Avenue
Memphis, Tennessee 38117

T HE PURPOSE OF MY SURVEY
was to discover how teenagers become Christians. When I began
this study over two years ago, I hypothesized a strong influence by
parents on faith acceptance among their teens. After interviewing
over 1,200 thirteen to eighteen year olds, I found that parental
influence is the number one predictor of teenage faith. Over fifty-
two percent (628) of the respondents cited one or both of their
parents as the major reason they became Christians.

What I was not prepared for was either the volume or intensity
of the teenagers' emotional outpouring of gratitude. I was deeply
moved as I read their expressions of profound appreciation for the
impact their parents had on their early faith experiences.

My mother is why I became a Christian. She showed me that I was
beautiful. Then she showed me that Jesus was the only way. . . . My
mother gave me life.—SHARI, 13

I was raised in a good Christian home with parents who accepted
Christ shortly before I was born. I have been attending church ever since
I can remember. So I guess I have grown up with the Bible. Around age
seven, I started asking questions at home. My mother told me the story

25

of Jesus and how to become a Christian. I understood, but waited. One Sunday evening in March of 1980, I couldn't sleep. I went to the living room and told my parents I wanted to be saved. My father prayed with me, and I cried because all I could think of was Jesus on the cross for me. Never has a little girl felt so free and forgiven.—TANYA, 17

I came to Christ through my parents. That's something I'll always keep in my heart. They gave me a gift no one can ever match—Jesus Christ!

—JAMES, 15

Apparently James Dobson's "Focus on the Family" and other family-oriented ministries are not laboring in vain to turn the hearts of the parents toward their children. There seems to be a lot of evangelism going on in children's bedrooms every night.

I became a Christian at age five when my Mom told me about Jesus on my bed before I went to sleep.—MIKE, 14

When I was six years old, I prayed with my mother in my bedroom. We had gone through a little booklet presenting the Gospel and then proceeded to pray the prayer at the end.—MEREDITH, 15

How many thousands of times have Mickey Mouse and Big Bird looked down from their wallpaper worlds to observe the holy rendezvous between a mother and child doing spiritual business with eternal ramifications?

I came to Christ on my mother's lap when I was six. I hadn't been able to sleep that night and I knew I was a sinner. I was afraid to sleep because I knew if I died I wouldn't go to heaven. I just had to go and get my mother out of bed. I was crying and I asked her to pray for me. So she took me back to my bedroom and told me about Christ. Then she helped me to pray, and I remember the peace that entered my heart that night like it happened today.—LEAH, 18

Most teens named their mothers as the ones who brought them to Christ. It seems the hand that rocks the cradle also holds a Bible.

My mom led me to Christ on a big backyard swing when I was eight years old.—BETH ANN, 15

I became a Christian in Vacation Bible School when I heard my mom speak.—RON, 17

When I was six, my mother was teaching children's church. I raised my hand when she asked if anyone would like to be saved. That Sunday morning, my mother led me to Christ.—ERIC, 18

Dr. Craig LeCroy's 1988 study, "Parent-Adolescent Intimacy," found that mothers share a greater degree of closeness than do fathers for both preteen and teenage sons and daughters. His research revealed, however, that the father's friendship with the teen was a better predictor of positive behavior in the teen than was a close relationship with the mother.[1]

The teenagers in my study indicated a disappointingly small percentage of father intimacy on a spiritual level. Still, those few responses were inspiring.

My dad is a preacher. We went to his friend's house one night and I stole a few small books about Jesus because I liked the way they looked. Dad found out, took me back to the man's house, and made me return them and apologize. His friend forgave me, but more importantly, my dad forgave me. On the way home in the car, the Lord dealt with me, and my dad led me to Christ.—JERROD, 17

I became a Christian at age seven when I saw my dad get baptized. It is so important for a child to see his dad as the spiritual leader of the household. This doesn't happen much because of the 'macho-man' thing in America. I'm glad my dad 'fights to be weak.' He's the toughest man I know!—MARK, 15

I came to know Christ by my dad talking to me about being saved. The next Sunday I went to the altar and asked Jesus into my heart.

—PAM, 13

For some of the teens, the decisions they made for Christ in elementary school through parental influence have lasted without a "faith crisis."

I grew up in a Christian home with Christian morals and Christian friends. My conversion was not earth-shattering; I simply made a commitment to Jesus Christ when I was nine. It was a natural decision for me to make. I have never had the desire to be a part of the world, and I know that I owe it all to Him. He is my life and my life is His.

—KATHY, 15

Before I was saved, I cussed a lot. But one night when I was seven, I went to Mom and told her that I wanted to become a Christian. She talked to me for a while, and then I prayed for Jesus to take over my life. Now that I am saved I don't cuss or anything. And I haven't regretted being a Christian yet.—SCOTT, 14

When I was five years old, my brother and I asked my mom what this picture on the wall meant. It was of Jesus knocking on the door. She taught us both about the Lord and asked if we wanted to become Christians. We were saved that day and are still learning about Christ.

—PETER, 13

THE DECISION YEARS

Even though some of these teens have not yet felt the need to rebel against the religious values of their parents, the fact is that for most teenagers, adolescence is that period when an informed recommitment to Jesus Christ is crucial. A full seventy-nine percent of the adolescents in my survey who were originally led to Christ by their parents made a responsible (and often highly emotional) decision as a teenager to make the Christian faith their own.

Out of these 628 respondents, 496 felt the need for an "inner conversion" resulting in an owned faith instead of the hand-me-down religion of their parents. They responded "strongly agree" to the statement, "During my teen years, I made a conscious decision to make the Christian faith my own." A majority of those also answered, "strongly agree" to the statement, "As a teenager, I experienced a period of time when I doubted that I was a Christian."

When I asked them to express their recommitment experiences in writing, most seemed eager to share.

I was raised in a Christian home and taught what was right and wrong. Yet, I always knew that someday I would be tempted to fall away and lose sight of God—and I did. Not until my junior year in high school did it all come together and I came back to God. Now I'm a Christian because I want to be one.—CHRIS, 18

I came to know Christ through my parents when I was seven years old. But I didn't start really living for what I believed until I was a freshman in high school. I think I just tried to live as a Christian because that's what my parents wanted me to do, not because it's what I really believed. When I got to high school, I knew that I had to decide whether I was going to live for God or for myself. I have been lonely so many times in high school because I have had to stand alone for Jesus.

—KATIE, 16

Even though the majority of the teens appreciated their Christian family background, I was surprised that so many of them regarded their early faith as unauthentic. It seems that a large number of teens view as personally legitimate only that faith which they have chosen during adolescence.

I was eight years old and attending children's church when I accepted Jesus as my Savior. But it wasn't until my sophomore year that I understood what giving my life to Him really meant. I didn't rebel much before that, but I honestly don't think I was really a Christian back then.—DONNA, 16

I grew up in a Christian family, so everyone expected me to be a Christian. Actually, I faked everyone out at church with my fancy clothes and fake attitude. I never was a Christian until age fourteen at church camp when the speaker talked about "phony Christianity." I knew that he was speaking directly to me.—JIM, 15

I became a Christian last year. I had been baptized before and said that I was a Christian, but the truth is that I wasn't. Then I went to my best friend's church and committed my life to Christ.—ELLIOT, 17

AFFIRMATION EVANGELISM

Among the youth in this study who made decisions for Christ during their teenage years, only a handful (less than two-and-a-half percent) named their parents as the factor which led them to faith. Does this mean that when our children reach adolescence that we parents can no longer influence their decisions for Christ?

On the contrary, no one can do "affirmation evangelism" among teenagers like Christian parents can. Jim Petersen, in his book

Evangelism as a Lifestyle, says, "I have expanded my understanding of evangelism to include planting, watering, and cultivating as well as reaping. I have learned that evangelism is a process."[2]

Jesus reminds us that "one sows and another reaps. . . . Others have done the hard work, and you have reaped the benefits of their labor" (John 4:37, 38). Judging from the results of this survey, it is rare for parents to experience a reaping ministry with their own teenagers. But the act of reaping is only a part of the evangelistic process.

Petersen claims that there are two primary modes of evangelism in the New Testament. The first he calls "proclamation evangelism"—an action through which teenagers receive a clear presentation of the Gospel and a challenge to commit themselves to it. Chapters 6-12 of this book will deal with those "proclamation influences" that the teens in my study indicated were directly responsible for leading them to Christ, and will show parents how to augment each factor.

But seldom do parents experience success using proclamation evangelism with their teens. Many teens revealed the "preaching approach" as the reason for rebelling against the faith of their parents.

After I turned fourteen, I became very rebellious and caused my parents a lot of pain. I think that the main reason I rebelled was because I felt like my dad was shoving Christianity down my throat.

—TIMOTHY, 18

In *Passages*, Gail Sheehy labels adolescence as the "pulling up roots" stage and explains, "In the attempt to separate their view of the world from their family's view . . . they cast about for any beliefs they can call their own. And in the process of testing those beliefs they are often drawn to fads, preferably those most mysterious and inaccessible to their parents. . . . Religious disinterest is one of the easiest and quickest ways to separate."[3]

Christian parents who observe their teens beginning to separate from the faith are often tempted to "preach them back into line." Proclamation evangelism is a necessary part of reaching your teens for Christ, but do not expect them to receive it from you. We Christian parents must be careful not to drive our teens permanently away from the church by our spiritual badgering. I know one mother of six who saw all of her teenagers abandon the church for a while, only to be reclaimed one by one. "I still have the teeth marks on my tongue," she says.

The second mode of New Testament evangelism, claims Petersen, and the one which best fits the parent-teen relationship, is "affirmation evangelism." What is the affirmation of the Gospel? It is the process of daily incarnating and living out the Christian faith.

Seeing a sermon is usually far more effective for teens than hearing one from their parents. Paul Borthwick, author of *But You Don't Understand*, writes, "As a youth minister, I can say from much personal experience that *the example of the parents* [emphasis mine] is the single most important factor in building convictions into the life of the teenager."[4]

Teens rarely want to listen to reason or common sense. "The best witness from the adult world," says writer Tim Stafford, "remains a life that shows the love, the integrity, and the power of the Lord Jesus Christ."[5]

Although someone other than their parents "reaped" by leading the following teens to Christ, these testimonies reveal the significant impact of parents who do affirmation evangelism.

I was fortunate enough to have Christian parents who presented the Gospel to me more by what they did [emphasis hers] than anything else. They never forced Christianity on me, and later on it became natural for me to make it my own.—MINDY, 17

I've always wanted to be like my father. He is a minister and the best example of Jesus I could have.—CHAD, 15

I was sexually abused as a child and moved from foster home to foster home. One day I was told I was going to be adopted by a family with no children. My new parents were Christians, and I watched their beautiful lifestyle. They never put any pressure on me, but I have now decided to ask Jesus into my heart too. I knew that I wanted what they had.—SANDRA, 16

NOBODY DOES IT BETTER

Why do Christian parents make the best evangelists of their teenagers? There are several good reasons.

1. No one loves teenagers more than their parents.

Whenever I am away from home on a speaking trip, I call my

wife every night. It is not a chore that I have to try to remember. It is an instinct. For years I have found that I simply don't sleep well unless I am certain that our children are safely tucked in bed.

Last winter I flew to southern California to tape two special programs about teenagers for Dobson's "Focus on the Family." My anticipation surged as the other two panelists and I sat in a studio, waiting to meet this man renowned for his concern for the spiritual welfare of American families. I remember wondering what he would be like in person. After the recent devastating exposes of other Christian radio and television personalities, I had learned not to get my hopes too high. Still, I couldn't help but be excited when the door opened and he bustled into the studio a few minutes late.

"I'm so sorry," he said, "but I've been at the hospital with our daughter. She was in a car accident a few months ago and today is having surgery done on her hand."

Perfunctory hellos were exchanged, followed by a preliminary briefing on the program's format. Have you ever been talking with someone when you suddenly realized that only one of you was really there? It was obvious to me that Dr. Dobson was preoccupied. His manner was polite and his professionalism intact, but his eyes betrayed the whereabouts of his spirit. He was looking over the surgeon's shoulder and praying for his beloved, college-age daughter. The real Dr. James Dobson, psychologist and popular author, was a man that two children call "Dad."

During a break between tapings, an aide slipped into the studio and handed Dr. Dobson a note. He thanked the bearer, scanned the message, and broke into a grin.

I called across the room, "She's okay, isn't she?"

He simply nodded and widened his smile. He was back with us. His child was "safely tucked in."

You don't have to teach Christian parents how to worry night and day about their struggling teenagers. It's an instinct. No one else is as concerned about their salvation and Christian walk.

Could anyone love the Laurent teens as much as their mother and I? I have always had a fierce loyalty to them that defies any other explanation than simply that I am their father, and I love them. When they are maligned and harassed by the world, my reflexes have been known to do a brain bypass in defending them. As our children grow, each one finds friends with whom they often feel closer and confide in more than they do in their parents. But no man born of woman will ever love our teens more than I do.

2. No one can provide "continuity" for teenagers like their parents.

Christian parents are in it for the long run. Edith Schaeffer told me once that what she hated most about divorce was how it destroyed "continuity" for the children. Meaningful relationships that they had every right to depend upon were no longer there for them.

The Christian parent will still be there for the teen when other more provocative friendships have long since lost their shine.

It was almost as if the apostle Paul was thinking of the parent of a teenager when he urged Timothy to evangelize "at all times, whenever you get the chance, in season and out, when it is convenient and when it is not" (II Timothy 4:2, TLB). When their teenagers' rebellion has run its course, the Christian parent will still be there for them—"in season and out."

Martin Luther King, Jr., cried out in the sixties, "We will wear you down with our capacity for suffering." In the same way, parents marked by endurance and grace can wear down their teenagers' resistance to Christ with a love that will not let them go.

Every parent needs to have a copy of Robert Munsch's children's book, *I'll Love You Forever.* It's a "two-hankie" portrayal of the enduring nature of parental love and how it crosses generations. In the opening scene, a mother is rocking her new baby back and forth and singing a lullaby to him: "I'll love you forever, I'll like you for always, As long as I'm living, My baby you'll be."

My favorite scene occurs when the boy reaches his volatile teenage years. Although the mother finds his taste in friends and clothes and music very strange, she still slips into his room at night to gaze at her sleeping son. "She picked up that great big boy and rocked him back and forth, back and forth, back and forth. And while she rocked him she sang: "I'll love you forever, I'll like you for always. . . ."[6]

Parents make the best evangelists because when the teen begins to fall away from God and sermons no longer have an audience, "affirmation evangelism" continues.

Anna the prophetess was bound to see the Messiah face-to-face. "She never left the temple but worshiped night and day, fasting and praying" (Luke 2:37). We Christian parents have that same bulldog grip on the promises of Christ for the souls of our teenagers.

"Believe in the Lord Jesus, and you will be saved—you and your household" (Acts 16:31). No matter what things look like now, we are in it for the long run. "His love endures forever" (Psalm 118:2).

3. *No one sees the possibilities of the "eternal" for their teenagers like parents.*

Paul described the task of a Christian parent when he said, "So we fix our eyes not on what is seen, but on what is unseen. For what is seen is temporary, but what is unseen is eternal" (II Corinthians 4:18).

All teenagers seem to go through that stage when they focus only on the temporary, suffering from "myopia of the soul." There are times when their attention is totally given over to who is dating whom, what is being worn by how many, and where is everyone getting together after the big game. The closest they can come to comprehending "eternal" is the length of the week just before they get their driver's license.

I overheard the following conversation between a teenage son and his non-Christian father.

"What is life, Dad?"

"Well, son, life is going to college and getting a good education."

"Yeah, I guess that's my question, too. Why do I want to do that, Dad?"

"That's easy. So you can get a good job when you graduate and make a lot of money."

"That's what I'm asking. Why, Dad?"

"Well, so that when you get married someday your own family can have it even better than you do."

"But why, Dad?"

"Uh, well . . . I guess so that after you die, your children can go to college and get a good education!"

Christian parents know that there is much more to life than what is currently playing on the main theater screen of their teenager's mind. Such parents, who have survived their own teenage years, can see beyond the temporary to the eternal.

"What is life?" asked John of his first century listeners. His answer is the same for us and our teens today: ". . . that they may know you, the only true God, and Jesus Christ, whom you have sent" (John 17:3).

Anyone who has run track knows that a relay race is usually won or lost by the passing of the baton. The team that is best at passing the baton will be the winner. For our families, that baton is knowing Jesus Christ as Lord and Savior.

It really doesn't matter how fast my teen runs the race of life. Sure, I may have bragging rights in the neighborhood for a few days if he scores the winning touchdown, or if she is elected homecoming queen. But their souls will survive, though the earth itself be forgotten and lost in its orbit and changed into dust. As Taylor Caldwell wrote in *Great Lion of God*, "that which is the spirit never dies. It is immortal. Therefore, is not that man a fool who puts his faith in this world and its treasures? His destiny is not with them. . . . His destiny is with eternity."[7]

WHAT'S A PARENT TO DO?

Before you can do effective affirmation evangelism among your teenagers, you should consider the following advice.

1. Learn how to cope with guilt feelings.

"Forgetting the past and looking forward to what lies ahead, I strain to reach the end of the race. . . ." says the apostle Paul (Philippians 3:13, 14, TLB). Unresolved guilt can have a paralyzing effect on Christian parents. Constantly asking the question, "Where did I go wrong?" can render them useless for any future spiritual gains with their teenagers.

"No one wanted to be a father more than I," a friend confided meekly. "But I've failed. Maybe I tried too hard."

"Where did I go wrong?" a mother softly wept. "How could I have failed so badly? I'd always tried to be a good mother, always tried to do all the things we learn that we're supposed to do as Christian mothers. But then I thought, 'Maybe if I'd have spent more time with my children, maybe if I'd been more faithful in my devotions, maybe if . . .' "

"The fact is," writes Myron Brenton in *How to Survive Your Child's Rebellious Teens*, "that no matter how much love and concern you feel for another human being, no matter how much you may want to protect that being, that child of yours, your responsibility for

35

him or her is limited. It is limited by the fact that you are human, not superhuman, and that your child, too, is human—that is, far more complicated emotionally than to be the outcome solely of your influence as parents."[8]

It seems that to be a parent is to know excess. We tend to be too proud one moment and too discouraged the next. I have known parents who felt so much guilt over their teen's rebellion that they spent days pacing the floor and sleepless nights tossing and turning in bed. They hammer themselves with accusations until they are emotionally and physically drained. Edging closer towards a type of mental paralysis, they can't seem to make important decisions regarding their teen. Perhaps by overburdening themselves with guilt, they don't have to act. Guilt, in such instances, keeps them from having to face their painful relationship with a teen.

But there is hope for the Christian parent. Hebrews 10:22 says, "Let us draw near to God . . . having our hearts sprinkled [with Christ's blood] to cleanse us from a guilty conscience." I would have more hope for any future influence on your teen's spirituality if you left all self-imposed guilt behind.

Ask yourself, as counselors suggest, "Did I deliberately try to hurt my child?" The answer, of course, is a resounding, "No!" There really are no experts in the field of raising Christian teenagers. We're all doing this for the first time. And whatever "wrong" you have done so far, you did unknowingly and with the best of intentions.

Once when I was feeling particularly guilty for not keeping a promise that I'd made to one of my children, I found the following hand-scrawled note on my desk: "Forget about it, Dad. I forgive you. You are not God."

In order for you to be available for God to use you in your teenager's life, perhaps the first thing you need to do is forgive yourself. One mother, working through her guilt, said, "We have tried. We aren't alcoholics or monsters. We've never done anything on purpose to hurt him. It just hasn't turned out right so far. You can only do so much. Everybody's human."

2. Let your teen see Christ in you.

"Remember your leaders [parents], who spoke the word of God to you. Consider the outcome of their way of life and imitate their faith" (Hebrews 13:7). If "affirmation evangelism" is the process of daily incarnating the Christian life, then the parents' major task is to show their teenagers Jesus Christ at every opportunity.

A high school junior wrote, "I gave my heart to Christ in 1989. I just decided that I wanted what my friends had. I probably would have become a Christian much sooner had either of my parents lived by their standards instead of just talking about them."

On the other hand, a sophomore girl responded, "My mother was like a walking billboard for God. I guess I always knew that Christianity was true, because I couldn't help but see Jesus in her."

In Charles Sheldon's classic, *In His Steps*, a group of believers decide that before making any crucial decision, they will ask one question: "What would Jesus do?" Can you imagine the impact that such a question might have on your relationship with a teen if you asked it just before she walked in the door fifteen minutes past her curfew, or after you found a pornographic magazine in your son's bedroom? The ensuing confrontation might be marked more by reason than hot tempers and will stand a far better chance of leading to changed behavior.

If nothing else, by asking "What would Jesus do?" first, you compel your teens to recognize that you are taking the lordship of Jesus Christ seriously for your own life. Chances are that they will remember your efforts when their own "decision time" arrives.

3. Be prepared for God to change you as well as your teen.

"Forget the former things; do not dwell on the past. See, I am doing a new thing!" (Isaiah 43:18, 19a).

I have come to recognize God's sense of humor in the fact that two things always happen to me when I want Him to change one of my teenagers. First of all, He starts His work on them by changing something about me. Then, after I surrender to His plan, almost without fail He goes further than I have given Him permission to go.

C. S. Lewis compared this phenomenon to the man who invited a friend into his home to help him rearrange a few pieces of his furniture. Before he knew it, the friend was drawing up new blueprints, tearing down walls, and building new additions. Lewis said that God is just like that friend. We think that we have invited Him in to make our little bungalow cozier, but He has something totally different in mind. He wants to make a mansion out of us.

In the same way, I am certain that God wants to do something new within you, even as He works on your teenager. With that thought in mind, I asked the teens in my study to finish the following open-ended sentence: "If I could change one thing about my parents, it would be . . ."

Two responses came back with overwhelming regularity:

- that my parents and I could really talk to each other and
- if they love me, I wish they would have faith in me and not give up on me.

These answers, revealing the two areas in which parental changes could have the greatest impact on teenagers for Christ, are the subjects of the next two chapters. Feel like rearranging a few pieces of furniture?

CHAPTER
4

In One Era and Out the Other

Evangelizing Your Teen by Building Communication

Violence is what happens when fear or anger interferes with communication. When you are very angry or very fearful, your breath comes short, it's difficult to speak, or to speak sensibly. You have lost the ability to communicate; you have lost control.—H. SAMM COOMBS

The quieter you become, the more you can hear.—ANONYMOUS

Y OU ARE NOT THE FIRST Christian parent to be tested on a daily basis by your teenager. Church-related teens are not always so different from their non-Christian counterparts. They can be hyper-critical, incredibly self-centered, unappreciative, and as determined to pierce your sanity with their behavior as they are to pierce your eardrums with their compact discs.

One mother wrote, "My teenager is driving me crazy. She thinks I'm a bank—there's no end to her demands—yet when I ask her to do a simple chore, I have to remind her so many times that she accuses me of being a nag. She blasts her stereo, stays on the phone for hours, lies about everything, and makes me wonder if she's doing drugs, because one minute she's as happy as a lark, and the next she looks as if she's about to commit suicide.

"I tell myself, 'It's normal teenage behavior. Why don't I lighten up? I'll take a long, hot shower and forget my woes.' I reach up to the shelf for my shampoo—and it's gone. 'I'll kill her,' I think as I grab a towel and run, dripping up the stairs to retrieve my shampoo from the upstairs bathroom."[1]

The problem is that after you finally get your hair shampooed, you look in the mirror and realize just why those tresses are grayer today than they were yesterday. In *Five Cries of Parents*, Merton Strommen says that the single factor that drives parents to distraction the most is their teenagers' seeming unwillingness to communicate. Parents complain, "When I try to talk to them about sex, school, the future, or any other serious matter, all I get is 'Yeah, I know, I know.' "

Elizabeth Winship, who writes a syndicated advice column about teenagers, warns parents, "Who's kidding whom? You can talk to teenagers, talk at teenagers, talk about teenagers, but can you really talk with them?" Her own answer is not very encouraging. "Getting a parent's goat is an adolescent must. Trying to run their own lives, teenagers become masters at disrupting yours. They greet your pronouncements with silence, blank stares or haughty scorn."[2]

Yet when I asked the teens in my study to complete the sentence, "If I could change one thing about my parents, it would be . . . ," the most frequent response was "that my parents and I could really talk to each other."

Strommen's research revealed the same desire. Hypothesizing that close-knit families encourage religious faith in teens and that families grow close through good communication, he asked 2,000 youth to complete the statement, "I wish. . . ." The most oft-repeated response was: "I wish I could talk to my folks about some of my problems."[3]

Psychologist Joyce Vedral concurs. "Teenagers want to talk to their parents. In fact, they're dying because they can't. Most teens who commit suicide are those who feel they can't talk to either parent. Their feelings of loneliness and alienation bring about the ultimate despair."[4]

Although parents often read them as being uncommunicative, the teens in my survey demonstrated a deep longing for positive communication with their parents.

I would like them to ask what's going on in my life, because sometimes I want to talk. But I don't think they're interested—CHERYL, 15

When I do something wrong, I would like for them to be more understanding and listen to me when I try to explain.—BOB, 16

I wish my Dad didn't get so mad when he talks to me.—DAVID, 14

I wish they wouldn't use me as an excuse to fight with each other.

—SHANNON, 15

It would be great if they would stop twisting everything that I say into what they want to hear.—HEATHER, 17

I wish my mom would talk with me as much as she does with my best friend.—SANDI, 16

We have seen that the highest hope of Christian parents is that their children experience a vibrant Christian faith. If these parents want to be used by God as a part of the process for evangelizing their teens, then their primary communication task is obvious: to close the gap between the two of them.

We can begin to narrow this gap in two ways: first, by making an effort to understand our teens; second, by an honest appraisal of why we act the way we do as parents.

WHAT TEENS THINK ABOUT

We may think that we know our teenagers well, but often we do not actually understand what is troubling them. "Parents too quickly impose what they think is going on in the teen's mind," says Dr. Robert Coles, psychiatrist at Harvard University. "You've got to pause to hear what the teen really is seeing and feeling. Teenagers will tell you how they feel if you make the effort to pay attention. But you've got to suspend your interpretive zeal for a moment."[5]

USA Today surveyed 5,300 teens to find out what their top five concerns were. The wise parent will listen carefully.

Concern #1. Sexual choice issues (teen pregnancy, sex education, abortion and birth control)

You can count on most teenagers spending a large portion of their time thinking about sexual issues. But many of them fear that if they express their thoughts about sex openly to their parents, they will be misunderstood or even condemned.

I just can't tell my mother what I know about sex, because she feels that a girl my age shouldn't know about these things. If I bring it up, she always manages to change the subject.—EDWINA, 16

I wouldn't feel comfortable talking to them about it. Besides, I know

*almost everything already because of sex education in school. I have
already experienced having sex, too.—ALEX, 16*

Your teen's struggle with sexual issues will not be served by your
silence. I have seen adolescents deterred for years from God's best
plan because of their bad choices in this area. The Bible warns that
sexual sin is unlike any other sin with the potential of destroying a
life (I Corinthians 6:18; Proverbs 6:32), and most teen surveys
reveal that the majority of youth are sexually experienced.

If you judiciously decide that you want your teens to talk with
you about sex, I advise you to refrain from lecturing until you hear
their whole story. Overly critical parents who threaten their teens are
more likely to drive them to secrecy or even promiscuity. If you
hope to ensure your teenagers' virginity by promising instantaneous
death should they ever consider losing it, then whom do you think
they will confide in when they face sexual conflict? You can be
certain of one person who won't be bothered. More than one
clandestine abortion has been arranged without the knowledge of
the Christian parents.

Joyce Vedral observes that ". . . teens tend to communicate with
parents they can laugh and joke with, parents who will understand
no matter what they say. When I've asked teens why they choose
one parent over another to talk to, they invariably say they choose
the one who is calm, who behaves like a friend, and the one who
never says things like: 'How could you do that?' "[6]

Because sex is such an emotionally charged issue and is often
substituted for the word "love" today, a discussion with your teen
about sex can be a natural lead-in to a heart-to-heart talk about the
depth of God's love. I have been privileged to lead more teenagers
to Christ after conversations about sex than all other topics
combined.

Concern #2. Popularity

The need to be liked by their peers reaches its peak in the
seventh and eighth grades. Ages twelve through fourteen constitute
that period when peer influence is operating at its highest level.
Ordinarily, the adolescent experiences a very natural distancing from
the parent and bonding with peers.

Instead of resorting to some ill-advised power play for emotional control of a teen, the Christian parent should work with this God-ordained phenomenon. Needing intimacy with friends outside the home is an important step in the process of eventual emancipation and self-government. One tangible way for parents to expedite the process is to make room within the family circle for your teenagers' friends and begin praying now for God to draw at least one stable Christian peer into a close friendship with your teen.

Concern #3. *Appearance*

Gazing at his own reflection in a pool, Narcissus had nothing on most teens today. Whether they like what they see in the mirror or not, their preoccupation with it is certifiable.

If you plan on winning any battles in the area of your teenagers' appearance, forget it. They have a clear perception of what is acceptable among their peers, and you have as much chance of changing that as you do getting them to stop blaming you for the color of their eyes, the texture of their hair, or the size of their noses.

My kids aren't satisfied with ordering their own appearance; they insist on dressing me, too. Sometimes I think I'm the only forty-three-year-old Ken doll in America.

"Dad, you're not wearing that shirt with those pants, are you? One of my friends might see you!"

"Okay, Dad, now tuck your shirt in like this; then pull it part way out again and let it hang down over your belt—yeah, just like that. Now roll your pants up like I taught you, and you will be totally hot!"

Just be thankful that appearance is largely a non-issue when compared to your teen's faith walk. It is better to save whatever mental and emotional energies you have left for the real battle over your teenager's soul than to expend them on disputes over hairstyles and hemlines. Such quarrels are not worth the damage they do to the open contact you seek with your teen. Your best strategy regarding your teen's profile is to "take a low one" yourself.

Concern #4. *The fear of being humiliated*

For the teenager, the fear of suffering humiliation far outranks many concerns that adults assume trouble them the most. "One of the most common triggers of suicide in teens is a humiliating experience, like getting caught stealing," states Ann Epstein, a psychiatrist at Harvard Medical School. "A teenager's self-image is forming continually, and is very shaky. They tend to blow some things out of all proportion. And their sense of guilt is much stronger and more moralistic than in adults."[7]

Psalm 125:2 promises, "As the mountains surround Jerusalem, so the Lord surrounds his people." The Christian parent plays a similar role to those mountains for the emerging teen. The very idea that they were caught doing something bad, might, in the teens' minds, mean that they will always been seen as being bad. If they are embarrassed, they might sincerely feel that they will never attain their dignity again.

As the Lord surrounds His people, so Christian parents can provide that one refuge of acceptance that their teenagers can find nowhere else. The opportunity for a parent to point a teen toward the sufficiency of God's love and protection is never greater than when that teen has been humiliated and beaten down by the vagaries of life.

Concern #5. The death of a parent

It is probably a surprise to most parents that teens would rank the loss of a parent as one of their foremost concerns. But after considering that millions of children have already, for all intents, lost one parent via divorce, their anxiety over the possible loss of the parent with whom they are living is understandable.

Simply that you are alive and someone to be depended upon is of inestimable worth to your teenagers. They may not express it in ways that you would like to hear, but more than you realize, your teens are thankful just to have you around.

WHY PARENTS ACT LIKE THAT

I should have come home wearing a sign that read, "Teenagers, beware! Dad's in a surly mood!" After a worse than bad day, I was confronted by one of my teens requesting the family car—one hour after I had run out of gas because someone (and you know who you are!) forgot to put gas in that car after using it.

Just after my childish outburst, a sister of the perpetrator (and you know who you are!) shook her head and commented from the couch where she had passively viewed her father's interpretation of

Christian parenting. "Dad, I can't believe you. You should know better than to act like that. I mean, you write books about this stuff!"

My daughter had tendered a question that has always puzzled teenagers: why do parents act the way they do?

In his *Teenage Survival Manual*, H. Samm Coombs tells teenagers, "Before your parents became parents, they didn't act that way. When your father goes to work, he doesn't act that way. When your mother is with friends, she doesn't act that way. The only time parents act like parents is when they are with you! But that's okay, because the only time you act like a son or a daughter is when you are with your mother and father!"[8]

Coombs reminds us that most of us are parenting by a combination of our instincts and the questionable model handed down to us by our parents. We fuss and fume, snoop and nag, because that is how we perceive parents are supposed to behave. When we yell at our teens for their poor study habits, messy rooms, and blasting stereos, we somehow feel better because we think we have fulfilled our parental duty. It is not that we enjoy the role of adversary to our teens—being a tyrant can be exhausting. But it's part of the job description, isn't it?

Parenting by instinct and tradition will succeed occasionally because we are created in the image of God and, once in awhile, a vestige of His wisdom is bound to surface. But if parents consider the effect that our basic sin nature surely must have on our inherent behavior, then we must conclude that instinct provides a poor basis for parenting.

Christian parents will find the right foundation, especially for building communication with their teens, in God's Word.

WHAT'S A PARENT TO DO?

Scripture has guidance for parents who are open to learning how to communicate with their teenagers.

1. Avoid a judgmental attitude.

"Do not judge, and you will not be judged. Do not condemn, and you will not be condemned" (Luke 6:37). Perhaps you have never thought of this passage with regard to the way you would like your teenager to treat you, but it is both appropriate and encouraging.

I naturally am more critical of anyone who is critical of me. The chances are slim to none that I would confess my faults or disclose my innermost fears to someone who assured me only of their understanding. I need to know that you will accept me no matter what I tell you. Mere understanding is not enough. I need unconditional grace.

My teens are no different. Teenagers make ready targets for our arrows of criticism because our own faults are too easily seen in them.

Wise is the father who opts for restraint as he listens to his daughter share a story that reveals her humanity. Discerning is the mother who determines to say nothing pejorative when her son confides in her.

Teenagers who perceive their parents as too judgmental are apt to resolve never again to make the mistake of giving those parents access to the private world of their thoughts.

2. Fathers must take time to build intimacy.

"Follow God's example in everything you do just as a much loved child imitates his father" (Ephesians 5:1, TLB).

Strommen's "Adolescent-Parent Study" revealed that over fifty-three percent of American teenagers spend less than thirty minutes a day with their fathers, and forty-four percent spend less than thirty minutes with their mothers. The most alarming revelation was that one-fourth of the ninth graders in the study spent less than five minutes a day alone with their fathers to talk, play, or just be together. It is no wonder that forty-six percent of the fathers surveyed admitted that they worry "quite a bit" or "very much" about how their teens feel about them. [9]

Family research has tended to focus on family interactions as measured by the amount of "talk time" between parents and their children. Walker and Thompson argue that "when researchers fail to differentiate between time spent with the teen and intimacy, they assume that quantity of interaction is the same as quality of interaction and that material exchange is the same as emotional exchange."[10]

Recent studies document that parents can have more influence on their teenagers than peers do, depending on the degree of intimacy felt by the teens for their parents, especially for their father.[11] Research shows that fathers, and not mothers, are perceived by their teens as lacking the ability to experience intimacy with them.[12]

In one study the sons viewed their fathers as "not being very understanding" of them, and the daughters rated them even worse—far behind teachers!—in their ability to share in a satisfying interpersonal relationship.[13]

Concluded the researchers, "Fathers, on the average, offer their daughters little or nothing in the way of intimacy, and the father-son relationship faces much turmoil during adolescence."[14]

The record reveals that teenagers can be affected for eternity by a Christian father who risks intimacy with them. Excusing yourself from emotional involvement with your teens by citing your choleric temperament, family background, work schedule, ad nauseum, is neither acceptable nor honest, and will do nothing to bring your child closer to Jesus Christ.

3. Mothers must not give up.

"Let us not become weary in doing good, for at the proper time we will reap a harvest if we do not give up" (Galatians 6:9).

Let me offer a word of encouragement to the mother who is praying her teen toward God without the help of a Christian husband. The single parent holds a special place in God's heart. You would not be the first one that He rescued by sending a Christian friend to influence your teen for God.

One such mother wrote, "When my son was a teenager, I found a note he had scrawled to himself in his bedroom, 'God, please help me!' I held the scrap of paper in my hand and felt hot wires of helplessness snap around my heart. I knew, because I was held back by his stiff resistance to my love, that I could not help him directly. I had completely run out of resources and could only pray, 'God, please help me!' God came to me in the form of a Christian police sergeant who befriended my son and asked him to go fishing. Angels are not as popular as they used to be, except on Christmas cards. But too many of them have moved people and events in my direction for me to doubt their existence."

Prayer can do anything that God can do, and your prayers are able to marshal the same resources from Him that this single parent received. "The Lord is close to the brokenhearted and saves those who are crushed in spirit" (Psalm 34:18).

4. Focus on the essentials.

"There is really only one thing worth being concerned about. Mary has discovered it" (Luke 10:42, TLB).

Paul Borthwick relates a conversation between a Christian father and his son who just asked for the car keys.

"Sure, you can have them," said the father, "under three conditions. First, you must clean up your room; second, you must read your Bible every day for the next month; and third, you must get a haircut."

The boy agreed, a month passed, and he appeared before his father. His room was immaculate and he could document a month's reading in the Scriptures, but his hair was still uncut.

"Well, Dad," he said hopefully. "I've done what you asked. Can I have the keys to the car now?"

The father replied, "I thought I told you to get a haircut first."

The son smiled brightly and offered, "Oh, yeah—that. Well, when I was reading through the Gospels this month, I realized that Jesus had long hair, so I thought I should follow Him!"

The father thought for a moment and, not to be outdone, retorted, "Good for you! Jesus walked wherever he went, and so will you!"

The father's sense of humor notwithstanding, the above conversation illustrates a preoccupation with nonessentials that severely limits communication with our teens.

Borthwick recommends that whatever the issue—music, movies, friends, dress—parents should first ask themselves the question: "Before I make a big issue out of this, am I sure that my teen understands the key issues of faith?"

"It seems a shame," he states, "when teenagers are crystal clear about why a Christian should never drink alcohol or should never dance, but are incapable of explaining the plan of salvation to a friend. Somewhere along the line, somebody got priorities confused as to what the most important convictions really are!"[15]

5. Do not compromise your own faith to reach your teen.

"Do not move an ancient boundary stone set up by your forefathers" (Proverbs 22:28).

While attempting to focus on the essentials and let non-issues pass without confrontation, the temptation might arise for sympathetic parents to join in their teens' temporary hiatus from the faith. Even though the rule of thumb for communicating with teenagers is, as Charles and Andy Stanley wrote, "to keep your kids on your team,"[16] teens searching for identity must know that their parents will not compromise their own Christian convictions.

Raised by parents with a *laissez faire* approach to religious and moral standards, one Harvard sophomore summed up his dilemma in personal terms: "In modern American society, particularly in the upper middle class, a very liberal group, where I'm given no religious background, where my parents always said to me, 'If you want to go to Sunday school, you can,' where they never forced any arbitrary system of values on me—what I find is that with so much freedom, I'm left with no value system. In certain ways, I wish I had had a value system forced on me, so that I could have something to believe in."[17]

This statement provides a vital clue for adults who waver in providing leadership. Whatever Christian parents do, they must graciously stand for God. Loving parents, standing their ground, can be a compelling influence for teens to find their own Christian values. Even in the heat of battle, when parents are short on grace and long on stubbornness, all is not lost.

Roger Paine writes, "The parent and teenager who can get mad at each other, who can level with their feelings and exchange hard words if need be, are often closer than the parent and teen whose relationship is one of carefully measured consideration."[18]

Such a confrontation might not be God's best plan, but even anger is better than apathy or polite tolerance. Between a parent and child, there is no monster like silence. It grows even faster than a teenager, filling first a heart, then a home, then a family history.

6. Don't assume that your teens are not interested in spiritual things.

"He has also set eternity in the hearts of men" (Ecclesiastes 3:11b).

Even the most visibly alienated teenager is reachable. Detective Myrle Carner, who spent eight years investigating criminal cases involving juveniles, reports that "Many troubled kids I speak with, especially those with uncertain futures, are looking for a genuine spiritual dimension in their lives."[19]

Let Christian parents be encouraged. Because teenagers have

been created in God's image, they are "inescapably self-conscious and inescapably God-conscious."[20] No teens will find rest for their souls or answers to their search until they find them in God. The apostle Paul reminded the non-Christians in Athens that, if they were sincere in pursuing the truth, their very roots in Creation must lead them to Jesus Christ. "In [God] we live and move and have our being. . . . 'We are his offspring' " (Acts 17:28).

No matter what the situation looks like now, your teens possess a natural receptivity to spiritual truth that you can count on. They have been created in the image of God.

GETTING PRACTICAL

Before a teen can receive spiritual truth, communication lines with a parent usually need to be restored. Following are some practical ideas on how to do that.

1. Don't jump to conclusions.

If you're suspicious about a certain situation, make a sincere effort to gather as much information as possible before drawing any conclusions. Parents have a tendency to overreact on the basis of insufficient evidence and then to "fill in the gaps" by assuming the worst.

2. Respect your teenagers' privacy.

You have no more right to read their personal letters, listen in on their phone conversations, or search their rooms to satisfy your suspicions than they would have to violate your privacy. Your rationalizing devices may tell you that it is your responsibility as a parent to know everything you can about your teen, but God never does a right thing the wrong way. Knowledge gained deceitfully will solve nothing and only further alienate your teenagers.

3. Try to retain a sense of proportion.

The son who does not sit in the front pew taking notes is not destined to be an atheist. The daughter who has not done daily devotions for months will probably not turn out to be a drug addict. There is no need for you to panic or exaggerate the situation. Both God and time are on your side.

4. Avoid asking rhetorical questions.

Communication stalls when teens have to deal with a question that, even if taken seriously, can elicit only an impudent reply. If you were a teenager, how would you answer, "How many times do I have to tell you to stop that?" or "Why won't you ever listen?"

The one question that teens dread the most is, "What do you think you're doing?" If parents could detect their teenagers' thoughts when asked such a question, they might hear: *What do you mean, "What do I think I'm doing?" I know exactly what I'm doing. The problem is what do you think I'm doing? It doesn't matter what I'm actually doing, I'm in trouble because of what you think I'm doing.*

5. Dispense discipline that fits the offense.

Teenagers have an inborn sense of justice and are quick to recognize when they don't receive it. Few things block the lines of communication like parents who are overly severe with punishment. The father who grounds his daughter for six months because she came home an hour late is asking for the silent treatment.

6. Recognize their limited verbal skills.

Teens can be intimidated by parents who use their facility with words to win verbal confrontations. Wise parents speak on their teenagers' level (without talking down to them) and understand that most adolescents, particularly boys, have difficulty describing their emotions.

One father found that simply asking a question like "How do you feel about . . . ?" opened up new dimensions in conversation. He tried this technique with his ninth-grade son, asking him about his feelings regarding a disturbing situation at school. To the father's amazement, the son answered on that level—talking about his feelings.

"It was wonderful!" said the father. "We talked for two hours! That's never happened before."

7. Make bedtime a sacrosanct occasion for communication.

The parent who decides that there will be time, regular, consistent, and—barring flash floods or nuclear holocaust—guaranteed, must still find an interval in the day for communication.

Our family ties up a lot of loose ends at bedtime. It may take more than an hour for my wife and me to go from room to room, almost like psychiatrists getting the day's rundown from our patients, preparing each child's path to sleep. During that time, when our children lie like small patients in the semidarkness, a great deal of what is on their minds and hearts, which the busyness of the day had kept suppressed, gets released. Each child knows that we are his or hers to talk to, without competition from siblings. It is important to us to know what is on their minds—it helps us to know what should be on ours. Perched on each other's beds, we discuss the issues that we never seem to find the right time or atmosphere for during the day.

8. Keep listening.

One of a parent's hardest tasks is to sit and listen to outrageous accusations. "You're only happy when I feel miserable!" "If you and Mom are right, you're the only parents who are!" Your instincts tell you to get defensive and engage the emoting teen in battle—but discretion keeps you from blurting out words that later you would wish you could retrieve. The onus is not on you to agree with the accuser, just to listen.

Communication between parents and teens is not the piling up of words; it is more of an attitude. When you resolve to do your best to understand who they are and why they act the way they do, when you decide to trade in your critical spirit for restraint and a listening ear, when you learn that nothing they do or say is important enough to cause you to withdraw your love, then communication that might lead to their salvation has begun. The next chapter reveals what the content of that communication must include.

CHAPTER
5

Have Faith in Me!

Evangelizing Your Teen via Trust and Forgiveness

*The reason children and their grandparents get along so
well is that they have a common enemy.*—MARGARET MEAD

WHEN I ASKED 1,200 TEENS TO
finish the sentence, "If I could change one thing about my parents, it
would be. . . ," their responses were almost evenly divided between
"I wish that we could talk to each other" and "If they love me, I wish
they would have faith in me and not give up on me." In Chapter 4
we addressed the first concern; in this chapter we will look at the
second.

Teen Magazine asked 2,300 adolescents, ages thirteen to
nineteen, from fifty-nine countries to pick three things that would
bring them the most happiness. From a list of eleven choices,
including fame, freedom, and a high-paying job, sixty-nine percent
of U.S. teens (sixty percent overseas) selected love. (Fame finished
last.)[1]

As encouraging as this sounds, my concern is that most adults
will misinterpret what love from a parent looks like to a teenager.

"I can't believe that my teen acts like she hates me sometimes,"
writes a pastor from Chicago. "I mean, how can she hate someone
who loves her as much as I do? Who worries about her more than I
do? What father pays more attention to his daughter? I tell her that I
love her every day."

Although it is important to verbalize your love to your children,

I am learning that for most teens it is a greater compliment to be trusted than to be loved. Because Christian parents tend to be rules-oriented, we think that we are showing our teens how much we love them by keeping them on a short leash, carefully monitoring their every move. Whether motivated by a genuine affection for our teens or not, overprotection is not perceived as love by a teenager.

Nothing erodes a parent-teen relationship like the drip-drip-dripping of distrust. No matter how often we give voice to our love and concern for them, teenagers are rarely convinced that it is love unless it is accompanied by healthy amounts of trust and respect. In the American Chicle Group's 1987 poll of 1,000 adolescents, teens chose "to be treated as an adult" as the number one ingredient for improving their home life.[2] The youth in my own survey concurred.

How will my parents ever know when I'm grown up? Whenever I ask their permission to do anything, all they ever say to me is, "You're too young."—BOB, 15

I wish my parents would stop treating me like I'm four years old. They are suffocating me.—ALLISON, 16

I want my parents to like my friends, but my dad, especially, treats them like dirt. He is too protective and always suspicious.—STEPHANIE, 15

I want my parents to treat me more like an adult and to stop talking down to me when I do something wrong.—SHANNON, 14

My dad is like a Nazi storm trooper! His way is the only way. How come I have no say in the rules at my house?—SEAN, 15

My parents never ask me if I have my own plans when they tell me I have to baby-sit my little brother. They only care about what they want to do. And they don't even pay me! —DENISE, 16

I know that my parents don't trust me. I can hear them pick up the phone when I'm talking to my boyfriend.—JANICE, 15

TRUST: AN INSTRUMENT FOR EVANGELISM

I have a student who became a Christian because, at a time when no one believed in him, he was trusted by an authority figure. In a fit of rage, his own stepfather called the president of our college to inform him that the student was a worthless liar and should be suspended. Later that day, shaken by this personal attack on the underclassman's reputation, the college president appeared at the door of his dormitory room.

Without asking the young man to defend himself, he simply related the stepfather's words. Then he read a verse from Scripture. " 'Can a mother forget the baby at her breast and have no compassion on the child she has borne? Though she may forget, I will not forget you!' says the Lord" (Isaiah 49:15).

With tears in his eyes, the president said, "Even though your own father has no faith in you right now, I want you to know that I do believe in you. No matter what you've done in the past, your record is clean at our school."

Those words of trust changed that student's life for eternity. Later, after publicly confessing Christ Jesus as Savior and Lord, he told me, "I don't think I would have ever become a Christian if that man hadn't believed in me even when I couldn't believe in myself." That young man went on to become president of our college's student body and today is in full-time Christian work.

Still, placing trust in a teen can be a formidable task for the Christian parent. When they are small, our faith in them springs as naturally as the love we feel for a new baby, in whose miraculous birth we play a large role. But as they grow into adolescence and begin to separate from us, having faith in them is increasingly difficult in direct proportion to the strength of their wills. Before parents can hope to build trust in their teens and thereby prepare them for their own trust in Jesus Christ, they must understand what trust is and what it is not.

What Trust Is. Humanly speaking, trust is your confidence in your teenager's potential to react maturely when confronted with life's pressures. I use the word "potential" because a parent must allow for a certain amount of failure. Self-government does not come without its share of trial and error.

Spiritually speaking, trust is your confidence in the Holy Spirit's ability "to keep [your teens] from falling and to present [them] before his glorious presence without fault and with great joy" (Jude 24). You are a Christian parent; you have resources that you have only begun to tap.

The Bible says that Job "prayed a hedge" around his children on a daily basis and expected God to watch over them (Job 1:5, 10). I do the same every morning without fail, and draw inner peace from the promise given in Philippians 1:6: "Being confident of this, that He who began a good work in [our teens] will carry it on to completion until the day of Christ Jesus."

What Trust Is Not. Trust is not having faith in your teen's natural goodness. No Christian parent should be so naive as to place unlimited trust in a teenager merely because some "experts" advocate a permissive parenting style. You don't have to be a parent for long to realize that the apostle Paul was right and the "tabula rasa" theorists wrong—no child is inherently good, possessing a "clean slate" at birth. When little Walter whacks another child in the sandbox with his shovel—without provocation—Paul's words that we were "born with evil natures" (Ephesians 2:3, TLB) ring true.

When Christian parents decide to trust their teenagers, they do so in full knowledge of their children's sinful nature. Such trust bestowed is not blind faith; it is a precious gift.

Giving undeserved trust does not mean putting up with behavior that is clearly unacceptable. The parent who avoids confrontation with a teen by removing rules and consequences has little grasp of the biblical concept of trust. Paul said, "Now it is required that those who have been given a trust must prove faithful" (I Corinthians 4:2). One Christian father, whose son had tried to sneak back into the house in a drunken stupor, greeted the teen at daybreak with a month's list of chores and a graded schedule for restoring him to the trust level he had violated.

"Cheap trust is not trust at all," said the father. "I wanted my son to know two things: that I loved him, and that there are consequences for making bad choices."

King Solomon learned an important lesson from raising teenagers of his own. "When the sentence for a crime is not quickly carried out, the hearts of the people are filled with schemes to do wrong" (Ecclesiastes 8:11).

The truth is that trust is both a gift and it is earned. Trust is occasionally strict and occasionally lenient, depending on the circumstances. There are times when a teenager "must prove faithful," but the wise parent remembers that a broken trust must not stay broken forever.

WHAT'S A PARENT TO DO?

1. When in doubt, believe your teen first.

"If you love someone you will be loyal to him no matter what the cost. You will always believe in him . . ." (I Corinthians 13:7, TLB). When you are faced with the choice of believing your teen's account of a story or the report of someone outside your family, believe in your teenager first.

I know a thirteen year old whose two best friends accused him, as a joke, of threatening them with a knife in social studies class. The principal did a cursory investigation and was about to call the boy's parents when a teacher came to his rescue with the truth. The student was relieved and grateful because, he told the teacher, "There is no way my dad would have believed me over those other guys, and I don't know what he would have done to me."

Nothing is more tragic than the teenager who reasons, "If my parents think the worst of me anyway, I'll simply live down to their expectations." A reversal of that philosophy has won more than one teen to the cause of Christ. "I became a Christian," said a preacher's son, "because my dad trusted me when I was untrustworthy."

2. Teach them to be responsible.

"Fathers shall not be put to death for their children, nor children put to death for their fathers; each is to die for his own sin" (Deuteronomy 24:16).

Distrust is both the form and the substance of "smother love." Parents who practice this misdirected type of love will not give their teens the opportunity to grow through accepting responsibility for their choices. They unwittingly defend their teenagers and cover up their mistakes by blaming bad friends, bad teachers, bad books, and even bad luck. If it is true that teens want to be treated like adults, then parents could save themselves a great deal of anxiety by complying.

If your daughter is habitually late for school, causing all of you to start each new day in a bad temper, calmly make the following announcement: "I won't be driving you to school anymore, dear, when you miss the bus. Neither will I be signing your excuse notes."

When your son consistently refuses to do his homework, forego the nagging and dispassionately state, "We're not fighting about your homework anymore. I'm willing to help when you really need me, but from now on it's up to you to get it done."

Such an approach does not mean that you are giving up on your teens. On the contrary, allowing them to suffer the consequences of their own mistakes is a compliment; giving them responsibility for themselves is a sign of trust.

3. *Make your rules few, clearly stated, and reasonable.*

"Come now, let us reason together . . ." (Isaiah 1:18).

"It's not the rules, Dad," pleaded one of my daughters during a lively confrontation. "It's your obsession with them!"

I grant that guidelines are important during the teen years, but their necessity does not give a parent license to establish a totalitarian regime with a rule for everything. Teens respond best to a parenting style that is neither too permissive nor too overbearing.

A study of students between the ages of fourteen and sixteen, conducted by Terrance Olson at Utah State University, revealed that teenagers are far more likely to delay their first sexual experience if their parents are only moderately strict. The teens most anxious to experience premarital intercourse were those with either permissive or very strict parents. "The least sexually active teens," reports Dr. Olson, "were those who considered their parents slightly more than moderate disciplinarians."[3]

At our house we hold periodic family pow-wows to discuss any rule changes needed in about eight basic areas (dating, curfews, chores, bedtime, church participation, etc.). During these discussions, we make a sincere effort to hear our teens' opinions and use their input to help shape the rules, for experience has shown that they are more likely to abide by guidelines in which they have an investment.

The parent should make certain that the rules are clearly understood by all involved. Many an argument has escalated when the teen insists, "But you never said. . . ."

4. *Look for opportunities to treat your teen as a contributing Christian peer.*

"As iron sharpens iron, so one man sharpens another" (Proverbs 27:17).

A good friend of mine closed a personal letter to her sixteen-year-old daughter, who was at a "spiritual crossroads," with these words of wisdom: "Sometimes I look at you and think, 'She doesn't realize who she is or what incredible things she could do for God's kingdom.' But Satan does realize who you are, and believe me, he fears that you will turn your firepower on him. I predict that during these next couple of years, you're going to come into your own as a Christian and put the rest of us to shame. So welcome to the adult world, sweetie. We've been waiting for you. And God knows how much we need you."

Few phenomena launch a teen toward self-government and responsible Christian commitment like a sincere invitation from parents to join them in a relationship of mutual accountability to the Christian faith. Because of their penchant for honesty, teens make natural exhorters and give penetrating advice when encouraged to offer their spiritual insights.

Someone once said that the reason Jesus told us to love our enemies was because they are the only ones who will tell us the truth about ourselves. Parents of teenagers don't need enemies to point out areas where they need to grow.

The older our teens get, the more we ask them for their help in solving anything from family problems to knotty ethical issues. To be made privy to the adult Christian world is a valued endorsement to teenagers and can serve as a catalyst for their own tenuous faith.

5. *Recognize the purpose for and limitations of rules.*

"The law was added so that the trespass might increase" (Romans 5:20a).

I am probably not the only Bible professor who has difficulty living in the home what I teach in the classroom. One evening last fall, after a stimulating class discussion on "law versus grace," I returned home to have dinner with my family. At the meal's end, one of my teens and I stayed at the table to clear the air regarding an infraction of one of the house rules.

With jaw set firm, I stubbornly insisted that any problems he had with me would disappear if he would simply abide by the rules. If I had stopped to measure that strategy against biblical theology, I'd have branded myself a heretic, but who takes time to think when trying to win an argument?

It was a combination of my son's tears and integrity that changed my mindless authoritarianism. "Dad, you just can't push me like this," he entreated. "I wish I could be what you want me to be, but I can't. When you tell me that I can't do something, it

59

makes me want to do it! If you keep pushing, I don't know what I'm going to do."

For an instant I couldn't breathe. God was at our dinner table at a rare moment when I was listening. I had heard my son's words that same day in class: "For what I do is not the good I want to do; no, the evil I do not want to do—this I keep on doing" (Romans 7:19). My confidence in the rules at our house was neither biblical nor very helpful. In fact, my passion for enforcing them was almost certainly driving my teen toward aberrant behavior.

In my zeal to be a Christian father, I had forgotten that the purpose of the law is to lead the teenager to the grace of the Lord Jesus. "So the law was put in charge to lead us to Christ" (Galatians 3:24a). Rules do not subdue sin; they increase it. Paul might have been a teen pleading with his own father when he said, "But sin, seizing the opportunity afforded by the commandment, produced in me every kind of covetous desire. . . . When the commandment came, sin sprang to life" (Romans 7:8, 9).

Although a moderate number of rules are necessary, the Christian parent should not be surprised if resistance to them rather than conformity is more than an occasional occurrence. You can depend upon a certain amount of rebellion, especially if the rules are arbitrary, endless, and enforced with severity. You cannot expect an intricate system of laws to produce a godly home.

God never meant for the Christian family to be centered around a list of rules and regulations. The law cannot mold a teenager into a responsible, inner-directed Christian. Just the opposite is true. It is "the grace of God that . . . teaches [teens] to say 'No' to ungodliness and worldly passions, and to live self-controlled, upright and godly lives in this present age" (Titus 2:11, 12).

Rules have done their work when our failure to keep them brings both teen and parent to the foot of the Cross, when they cause each family member to cry out with Paul, "What a wretched man I am! Who will rescue me from this body of death?" (Romans 7:24). Our answer must be the same that Paul gave. Our rescue comes through the grace of our Lord Jesus Christ.

Teenagers are not only crying out for better communication and to be treated like adults; they also want to know that when they fail, you will not give up on them. The measure of grace that you show them might be the factor that "teaches [teens] to say no to ungodliness."

The most passionate part of Garrison Keillor's book, *Lake Wobegon Days*, is his "Ninety-five Theses on Childhood." Written by a native son who escaped to a large city, the ninety-five theses document the psychological ravages of being raised in an ultra-strict, religious home in small-town Minnesota. He cries out to his parents:

> *You have taught me to feel shame and disgust about my own body, so that I am afraid to clear my throat or blow my nose.*
>
> *You have taught me to worship a god who is like you, who shares your thinking exactly, who is going to slap me one if I don't straighten up.*
>
> *You have taught me an indecent fear of sexuality. I'm not sure I have any left underneath this baked-on crust of shame and disgust. . . . A year ago a friend offered to give me a back rub. I declined vociferously. You did this to me.*
>
> *Guilt. Guilt as a child, then anger at you for filling me with guilt, then guilt at the anger.*
>
> *But most of all, because you could never forgive me—for not being as intelligent as your other children, for not being the right sex, for coming at the wrong time in your life, for just not measuring up to your standards—I don't know how to forgive my own children.*

Keillor concludes this furious catalog in answer to the parental complaint, "Why don't you call us anymore?" with these bitter words:

> *I don't call you because I don't need to talk to you anymore. Your voice is in my head, talking constantly from morning to night. I keep the radio on, but I still hear you and will hear you until I die.*[4]

Forgiving Your Teenager

People who know little of what it means to be forgiven find it is almost impossible to forgive others. If teenagers are ever to know the love of Jesus Christ, then they must experience being forgiven.

Of the woman who anointed His feet with perfume and wiped them with her hair, Jesus explained to the self-righteous and guilt-ridden Pharisees, "Her many sins have been forgiven—for she loved much. But he who has been forgiven little loves little" (Luke 7:47).

Parents who find it impossible to forgive their teenagers cannot expect to see their children drawn to a religion characterized by legalism and intolerance. Neither will those parents experience the inner peace and clear conscience that come from having their own sins pardoned by the heavenly Father. "If you do not forgive [teens] their sins, your Father will not forgive your sins" (Matthew 6:15).

I received a visit from a Christian father who told me that he was tired of not being able to sleep and that he had to talk with me. His story was not unfamiliar. His daughter Abby, a high school senior with a promising future and a full scholarship to a Christian college, had disclosed to him two weeks earlier that she was pregnant. She had no desire to marry the child's father and had decided to get a job, have the baby, and abandon her plans for an education.

The father confessed to me, "I have been unable to deal with any of it. I just want it to go away. Inside I feel guilty, humiliated, and too angry even to discuss it. I know that I'm wrong, but I just can't talk to her right now."

Anger runs high among Christians because of their tendency to deny its existence. They reason that a good Christian must always appear loving, so they swallow their anger when it threatens to surface. I call it "sanctification by swallowing."

I warned my friend that if he persisted with that tactic, he was making his reservation for an early grave. He paused for a moment, then burst into tears and blurted out, "I hate her. I hate my daughter for what she's done to us!"

I gave him a brotherly hug and encouraged him to let it all go. For the next half hour he sobbed out his innermost feelings, and I believe he was shocked at the depth of his anger. But for the first time, he was ready to listen to reason and let God's Spirit begin to heal his emotional hurt.

I told him that there is hope, and that the key is forgiveness. I asked him to look up and memorize I Peter 4:8, because it is the most important verse in the Bible for maintaining the parent/teen relationship: "Above all, love each other deeply, because love covers over a multitude of sins."

Just how do you become a forgiving parent? Here are some tips.

WHAT'S A PARENT TO DO?

1. If the Sinless One could forgive, so can you.

"Be kind and compassionate to one another, forgiving each other, just as in Christ God forgave you" (Ephesians 4:32).

During His ministry, it seemed that Jesus spent almost as much time forgiving as He did teaching. He pardoned the woman caught in adultery, the disciples who betrayed Him, Mary Magdalene, His own crucifiers, and the thief on the cross. Many of His parables examine forgiveness—the prodigal son, the debtor servants—and one of His strongest warnings is that Christians first make peace with their brother or sister before laying their gifts before the Lord.

It is remarkable that the One who did nothing for which He needed to be forgiven, uttered the sublime words, "Father, forgive them" from the cross. If I can be forgiven for the most heinous crime of all, my sinful, self-centered nature which sent the Messiah to an ignominious death, then I can forgive my teens for their petty sins against me.

2. Look to Jesus and be healed.

"For he himself is our peace, who has made the two one and destroyed the barrier, the dividing wall of hostility" (Ephesians 2:14). The same One who forgave you from the Cross can remove the alienation between you and your teenager.

When Jesus said to Nicodemus, "Just as Moses lifted up the snake in the desert, so the Son of Man must be lifted up" (John 3:14), He was referring to an extraordinary story in Numbers 21. Once, when the children of Israel were throwing their weekly pity party and had forgotten again to invite God, He sent poisonous snakes to get their attention. After they prayed for deliverance, the Lord instructed Moses to fashion a bronze serpent and put it up on a pole. Then, of course, the people had three choices. They could continue to look at the snakes and curse them for their venomous assaults, they could focus on their own pain and curse their bad fortune, or they could obey God and look to the bronze serpent for healing.

It seems to me that the offended parent has the same three choices.

3. Remember the struggles of your own youth.

"Once you were less than nothing; now you are God's own" (I Peter 2:10, TLB).

I know parents who act like they have completely forgotten what it was like to be a teenager. We have grown so envious of our teens' unwrinkled skin, thin waistlines, boundless energy, and carefree outlook that we forget we wouldn't be teenagers again even if it meant that we'd have a full head of hair to comb and joints that didn't need a jump-start every morning.

Parents will more quickly forgive their teens if they remember that they too were once blobs of passionate protoplasm. All of us, as teens, were largely inarticulate, fearful of being laughed at, desperate to prove that we were worth something, prone toward skinniness or chubbiness, shy, clumsy, and terrible at fractions.

One of my teenage daughters has a poster by her bed that reads, "I don't feel grown up—I feel lousy!" Just underneath these words she wrote, "People need loving the most when they deserve it the least."

How could any parent who remembers what it is like to be a teenager possibly keep a grudge? If there is ever a time when a friend needs mercy, it's when he or she is a teenager.

4. See the offense as an opportunity to evangelize your teen.

"Do everything without complaining or arguing . . . as you hold out the word of life" (Philippians 2:14-16).

Jim Petersen, in *Evangelism as a Lifestyle*, claims that "ninety percent of evangelism is love. It is the love of Christ that compels us to become Christians. I have to admit I never saw much enduring fruit in evangelism until I began to understand the importance of this truth and began to put it into practice."[5]

Jesus said to the woman caught in adultery, "Has no one condemned you? . . . Then neither do I. . . . Go now and leave your life of sin" (John 8:10, 11). The Bible doesn't say what happened next, but I'm certain of two things about the woman Jesus pardoned. She became a Christian that day, and then she changed hobbies.

Parents can expect the same results with their children. The teenager who is forgiven much might become the same one who loves much. Few things reach teens for Christ like being forgiven by an offended parent.

One teen I know broke his parents' hearts by leaving home his junior year in high school and plunging into a degenerate lifestyle. After months of living out of a suitcase, the excitement of the party scene reached its ebb, and the prayers of his parents took effect. But he wondered if they would ever forgive him and let him return.

Too ashamed to ask their forgiveness in person, he wrote a letter and confessed his outrageous behavior. He told them that a friend would be driving him by the house sometime on Saturday, and that if they would forgive him and allow him to come home, they should hang the blue sheet from his own bed on the clothesline as a token.

That Friday night, the Christian mother went to her laundry room and embarked on a labor of love. When Saturday afternoon arrived, the prodigal drove by the house, wondering what their answer was. What he saw was every sheet in the house dyed blue and hanging from the clothesline! Such is the abundant forgiveness of God and affirmation evangelism at its best.

CHAPTER

6

The Church
as Evangelist

*The future of the church will rise or fall on its success
with its young people.—GEORGE GALLUP, JR.*

THIS STUDY HAS ALREADY
revealed that, although no one can do affirmation evangelism like
Christian parents, very few teens are directly led to Christ by their
parents. Now we turn to the influences which the teenagers in this
study cited as the immediate factors responsible for their accepting
the Christian faith.

Next to the influence of parents, the most encouraging results of
my survey of 1,200 teenagers was their response regarding the
church. In fact, when students between the ages of thirteen and
eighteen make a decision for Christ, the number-one factor
influencing their choice is the church. Over thirty-eight percent of
the respondents who became Christians after reaching their teenage
years cited the church as the major reason for that decision. Their
gratitude for the church was heart-warming.

*I love my church! I was searching for something, so I came and got
involved in the youth group and Bible study. I literally surrounded
myself with Christian happenings. Eventually, just from being there,
the Holy Spirit took over.—JESSICA, 16*

If I hadn't found a good church, I'd never be a Christian today.

—TIM, 17

Three things led me to Christ: an elderly Sunday school teacher who took the time to answer my questions, a pastor who preached a sermon called "Are You Sure You Have Eternal Life?", and my own growth from a disciplined study of God's Word.—PAT, 18

Many teens became Christians because of the authenticity of the believers they met at church.

My life changed when I met people who were genuinely excited about the Lord Jesus.—LAURA, 15

I was first exposed to Christianity when I took a baby-sitting job at a church. It was only a matter of months, after being surrounded by people who were full of God's love, that I realized my life needed some serious changes.—MICHELLE, 16

I came to know Christ as Savior after observing the lives of some Christians I knew at church. Week after week I watched them, and finally decided that what they had was what I needed.—TERRY, 17

Senior pastors played an important role in winning several of the teenagers to Christ.

I have a loving pastor, who listened to me and helped me find Jesus.

—TAMMY, 16

I became a Christian after the sermon one Sunday morning. I walked down the aisle to the pulpit where my big, compassionate pastor met me. He put his arm around me and knelt with me right in front of the church. It's there where I came face to face with Jesus.—BILL, 14

I came to Christ through my favorite person in the world, my pastor.

—RUSSELL, 13

I was saved through a very moving sermon from my pastor.—BRYCE, 14

A CHURCH THAT LOVES TEENS

For two decades, the general consensus among adolescent psychologists and church sociologists has been that as children enter their teenage years they are less interested in organized religion and therefore less likely to be influenced by the church. Search Institute reports that "most of our studies have shown a decline in interest in formal religion from younger to older adolescence."[1]

Psychologist John Conger sums up the findings of these studies: "Today's adolescents are placing more emphasis on personal rather than institutionalized religion. This is consistent with the greater stress among teens on personal values and relationships and on individual moral standards, with less relevance on traditional social beliefs and institutions."[2]

The problem with analyses like these is that they have a tendency to become self-fulfilling prophecies, putting even more distance between the teen and the church. Adult church leaders read them and lose a measure of hope for making significant gains for Christ among American teenagers.

This lack of vision is nowhere more evident than in most church budgets. Youth worker Dennis Miller reports that "the average local church allocates only two percent of its budget to youth ministry, while secular companies selling everything from makeup to pornographic magazines are focusing up to seventy percent of their advertising budgets on the teenage market."[3]

Stuart Briscoe creates a penetrating commentary on the present situation in his book, *Where Was the Church When the Youth Exploded?*

> *There are more of them than ever before. Healthier because of the balance of their diets. Wealthier because of the balance of payments. They travel more, see more, earn more, spend more, demand more, receive more. They are pandered to, planned for, pleaded with, and preached about. Cheering, jeering. Swinging, singing. Drug scene. Teen scene. Obscene. The whirling world of* YOUTH.
>
> *Meanwhile back at the Church . . . Preachers preach Sermons carefully, prayerfully prepared. Expositional. Exegetical. Dispensational. Devotional. Inspirational. Indigestible. Budget met. Baptistry wet. Tithers tithe. Choristers chorus. Well dressed. Well pressed. Well blessed. The placid world of* CHURCH.
>
> *Two worlds on one planet. The woolly weird Youth World. The calm, cool Church World. The "out of sight" world. The "out of touch" world. And never the two shall meet. But they must!*[4]

Illustrating the breach between the church and today's teenager, the Princeton Religion Research Center reports, "Less than one out of five teenagers expressed a high degree of confidence in organized religion. In fact, although seventy-one percent of this sample admitted to church membership, two out of three youth blamed the church for not reaching out to them. Over eighty percent believed that a person could be a good Christian without attending church. While seventy-five percent said they believed in a 'personal God,' less than one percent desired to pursue a career as a member of the clergy."[5]

That there is a mutual and somewhat natural withdrawal between the teenager and the church is a well-documented fact. That we regard this separation as inevitable is unacceptable. Briscoe was right; the world of the church and the world of the teenager must meet.

Gallup warns that "if the church does not respond, young people will find an agency, movement, or experience that does." He claims that within the last few years over twenty-seven million people, most under the age of thirty, have turned to cults of one form or another. "Clearly," cautions Gallup, "the deep spiritual hunger of young people is not being met by the established church."[6]

I have contended for years that the problem has never been whether or not teenagers will believe in the church. The problem is whether or not the church will believe in her teens. A pastor friend of mine regularly prays aloud in front of his congregation, "Father, make us a church that loves teens."

The pro-church responses of the teens in my study show that the potential is there. The church is still able to win teenagers to Jesus Christ. One of the many redeeming qualities of adolescents is that they respond to truth and life wherever they find it. If the church makes an honest effort to live up to the One for whom it is named, teenagers will answer His call.

THE FIVE CRIES OF CHURCH-RELATED YOUTH

One of the major theses of this book is that most teenagers experience a period of religious doubt. While critically evaluating their childhood beliefs, they reach a point when they must discover a faith that is their own, that time when they make a decision to come into the Christian faith or disengage from it. Having observed thousands of teens at this faith-crisis juncture, I have distinguished five common cries they are addressing to the church. A church that loves teens will listen carefully.

Cry # 1: "Let us know that you care about our needs."

For a couple of reasons I consistently encourage pastors to reserve the front pews of their churches for teenagers. First of all, it is next to impossible to speak in a stained-glass voice, spouting religious cliches in an other-worldly tone, when looking directly into the faces of several teens with their Bibles open. Both their vulnerability and penchant for honesty compel the speaker to preach to their needs with incisiveness.

Secondly, I've noticed a remarkable phenomenon, the truth of which should be noted by all homiletics professors. When the pastor's sermon makes contact with teenagers, it effectively reaches almost every age group. The reason for this is that most topics which interest teens have a universal appeal. When Scripture speaks to loneliness, depression, ethics, family relationships, death, sexual purity, self-esteem, etc., teens will not be the only group to become attentive.

A pastor in Iowa testifies, "Two teenagers from our church approached me last year with an interesting request. With positive attitudes, they said, 'Pastor, you know that we like you and we are really trying to get something out of your sermons. But most of the time we don't understand what you're getting at. Could you preach a couple of messages that speak to our needs?' I was genuinely touched by their request and told them I would do them one better. If they would pray for me, I would preach a series of messages specifically for them.

"A large number of teens began praying for me every Saturday night, and a wonderful thing started happening. Our whole congregation could see the change in me and in my sermons. I had been growing stale, comfortable, and bored with my own messages. Since they started praying for me and taking notes, I cannot tell you how excited I am to preach on Sunday mornings."

Of the 167 items in the questionnaire that I administered, the item which elicited the most negative response was, "Most sermons that I hear are quite interesting." Over ninety-five percent of the time, the teenagers answered "strongly disagree."

Another study done among teenagers who left the church

criticized organized religion for having lost "the real spiritual part of religion" and for being "too concerned with organizational as opposed to spiritual issues." Forty-nine percent agreed with the statement, "most churches are not effective in helping people find meaning in life."[8]

If the church is to reach today's teens, then it must speak to their needs.

Cry # 2: "Give us life and not meaningless rituals."

Ritual is necessary, even desirable, when it communicates, because it is a visible symbol of the Christian truth it represents. But when it exists as a formal and complete entity in itself, the truth it symbolizes and explains forgotten or unheeded, then it is an empty form. Such ritual is dangerous, especially among teenagers, because they are too honest to believe that it is true worship. Ritual on its own contains no life, and the church must convey life to make contact with the teen.

One of the healthiest things a Christian parent or pastor can do is attempt to see the services of the church through the eyes of a teenager. You might begin to verbalize the same questions they are thinking. "Why do normal people talk so differently when they get behind the pulpit?" "How can I 'lift my Ebenezer' while we're singing when I don't even know what it is?" "Why do people change their voices when they pray?"

Any biblical term that is not a part of a teen's everyday language needs to be translated. Some of the more common words that should be illustrated in practical ways for all church members are "justification," "reconciliation," "grace," "sin," "regeneration," and "walking in the Spirit." Terms that mystify teens are probably just as vague and confusing to most adults.

Cry #3. "We want to know more about Jesus, not religion."

Dr. James Kolar, in the book *Evangelizing Youth*, relates his own inspiring odyssey through the storms of youth ministry. He tells how he and his staff tried everything to reach youth, using whatever new strategy was in vogue to build a strong program for teens. For a while they thought the key was "self-image," then "communication skills." Later they went from "relationship building" to "values clarification" to "education based on the latest psychological and developmental theories." After experiencing a personal spiritual renewal, he realized that what he had been looking for all those years, the key to reaching youth, was nothing less than "the person and work of Jesus Christ."

Kolar states, "We began to see that the essential thing was conversion to the Lordship of Christ . . . the absolutely irreplaceable foundation upon which our lives and the lives of the young people we worked with had to be built. Since that time we have learned again and again that the real power to live the Christian life comes from that one foundation, the foundation of what God has done for us in Jesus."[8]

Kolar concludes his testimony with this clarion call: "The presentation of the Gospel message is not optional. . . . It is unique. It cannot be replaced. It does not permit indifference or accommodations. It is a question of people's salvation."[9]

Jesus Christ is the Gospel. He is the Message that teens must hear. It is possible to be involved in the machinery of Christianity without knowing Jesus in a personal way. One teenager wrote,

I went to church for three years but I was just going through the motions. Then a friend invited me to a retreat at his church. During the service, a group did a play in which they re-enacted the whole crucifixion scene and the events that led up to it. Later, they vividly talked about Jesus—who He was and what He had gone through for me. I became a Christian that night because for the first time in my life, I saw Jesus. I am eternally grateful to that church for showing me who He is.—BRANDON, 17

Most surveys are probably accurate when they find that almost ninety-five percent of American teens believe in God. But the difference between a mental assent to the existence of God and a salvation experience with the Lord Jesus Christ is the difference between spiritual life and death. Countless teens would decide for Christ if they could meet Him where they live and hear of Him in language they could understand.

The onus is on the church to reveal Jesus Christ to the modern-day teenager and to recognize what evangelizing youth is and what it is not.

Evangelizing teenagers *is not* simply:

1. *making teens better church members (even though that will result)*
2. *getting teens to believe the right things and behave in the right ways*
3. *getting inactive teens to return to the church*
4. *modeling the Christian life, hoping that teens will "guess" that Christ died for them*

Evangelizing teenagers *is*:

1. *interesting teens in Jesus Christ*
2. *informing them clearly about Jesus' person and work*
3. *informing them of their need for a conversion experience with Christ*
4. *introducing them to a personal commitment to Christ*
5. *initiating them into a daily, growing friendship with Christ*

The church's message, method, and motive must be Jesus Christ. Our teenagers are dying to meet Him.

Cry #4. "We want to know what the Bible means for us today."

From the results of his latest "Religion in America" poll, George Gallup observes a paradox. Although only five percent of teenagers do not believe in God and ninety percent pray on occasion, among churched youth only three percent can list the Ten Commandments, fifty percent can name the four Gospels, twenty percent don't know the number of disciples Jesus had, and less than one-third know who delivered the Sermon on the Mount! As Gallup concludes, "We revere the Bible, but we don't read it."[10]

There are a great many teenagers (and churchgoers in general) who, for all their churchianity, have never come to grips with a clear presentation of the Gospel. If they are to discover a faith that can endure the pressures they will surely face, then that faith must be founded upon the Bible and not merely on family or church traditions.

I met a young man last winter who had just finished a course entitled "Interpreting the Bible" at a liberal midwestern college.

Teaching from an anti-supernatural bias, his professor "demythologized" both testaments for the student and left him with a book that was no more authoritative than any other textbook.

"I will never read the Bible again," the student confided in me. "I don't even know if I'm a Christian anymore, or even what a Christian is. With no Bible, I have no frame of reference for my life anymore, no absolutes, no power."

Statistics show that church-going Americans are largely ignorant about the great doctrines of their faith. Pastors cannot afford to capitulate to the values and philosophies of contemporary society. With a recommitment to orthodoxy and a high view of Scripture, they must preach without compromise to those hungry for God's truth. Karl Menninger, psychologist and author of *Whatever Became of Sin?*, challenges all preachers: "We know that the principal leadership in the morality realm should be the clergy's, but they seem to minimize their great opportunity to preach, to prophesy, to speak out. . . . Some clergymen prefer pastoral counseling to the pulpit function. But the latter is a greater opportunity to both heal and prevent."

Dr. Menninger believes that preachers have a golden opportunity to impact people in their daily lives and for eternity. "How?" he asks. "Preach! Tell it like it is. Say it from the pulpit. Cry it from the housetops. What shall you cry? Cry comfort, cry repentance, cry hope."[11]

"My people are destroyed from lack of knowledge," declares the Lord (Hosea 4:6a). Teenagers make willing Bible students and are eager to find in the Scriptures authoritative answers for their lives.

Cry #5. "Call us to total commitment, not part-time membership."

"The arriving generation," claims George Gallup, "is more than hinting; it is screaming to be used in some demanding cause."[12]

I have noticed an encouraging trend among youth conferences across America. Ten years ago, the program committees spent a great deal of time trying to entertain the teens, keeping them busy enough with seminars and recreation that they wouldn't get into much trouble and possibly they might even learn something to take home with them. I always felt the challenge of trying to get their attention when I would deliver the evening address at those rallies.

A few years ago I began to observe a shift toward engaging the teens in mission projects and community service events: distributing food among the poor, visiting shut-ins, cleaning up neighborhoods. After having spent the afternoon being used by God to help someone less fortunate, the teens themselves changed the atmosphere of the evening programs. Several would ask permission to stand and share what God was doing in their lives.

For a recent youth conference in downtown Chicago, the program committee chose as its theme "Piercing the Darkness for Jesus Christ." Every morning the 750 conferees were trained; then every afternoon they were sent out to do New Testament evangelism on the city streets.

One might think that the average, self-conscious, tongue-tied teenager would balk at such a challenge. On the contrary, these teens formed a spiritual juggernaut that rocked the Windy City. Grounded in Scripture and inflamed by God's love, they sent spiritual shock waves from Watertower Place on Michigan Avenue to Pacific Garden Mission on State Street.

I have never felt so useless as a speaker in my life. They didn't need me to preach in the evenings. Their spontaneous testimonies of the miracles that God had performed that day in public parks and on city beaches could have gone on for hours. And when I did speak, their pens were poised and notebooks open, ready for further equipping to "go into all the world." I had to remind myself that these were average teenagers—except for one thing. They had received an invitation from visionary adults to "deny themselves, take up their cross, and follow Jesus."

If the church calls them to costly discipleship, it will find teenagers ready to follow a God who, as Dietrich Bonhoeffer said, "bids us come and die." In fact, we will not reach them if we ask them for less.

WHAT'S A PARENT TO DO?

1. Get involved in the church yourself.

"Each one should use whatever gift he has received to serve others" (I Peter 4:10).

Several teens in the survey expressed a deep desire for their parents to be active in the faith.

I wish my dad would enjoy coming to church. He only comes now and then because he feels like he has to.—MARTIN, 14

I am so envious of my friends who were raised in a good Christian home. As far as I know, my parents have never stepped inside a church.

—MARTHA, 17

If I could change one thing about my dad, I would have him care less about money and more about his faith.—CHAD, 16

Why should teenagers be expected to take their faith seriously when their parents do not? Research shows that they don't—especially when the prodigal parent is male. According to a survey done among evangelical teens in the Midwest, the father's attendance pattern has a significant influence on the frequency of church attendance by high school seniors.

If both the father and mother attended church regularly, over ninety percent of high school seniors followed suit. If only the father attended, a robust seventy-six percent imitated him. But if only the mother attended, the number of seniors who continued in attendance dropped off to an alarming twenty-one percent.[13]

Even Christian parents cannot simply attend a religious service once a week, sit politely in a pew for an hour, and expect their teenagers to commit their lives to the lordship of Jesus Christ. Parents who want to influence their teens' faith will seek out active involvement in a local church.

2. Encourage your teens to keep up their church attendance.

"Let us not neglect our church meetings . . . but encourage and warn each other" (Hebrews 10:25, TLB).

Many teens experience periods when they are less than enamored with the church. During those times, you can honor your teens' negative feelings without pandering to them. They may need you to listen, but they don't need you to sanction their withdrawal from the church simply because they would rather sleep in than study the Ten Commandments.

Accepting their feelings is a middle way between dismissing them and acting upon their every complaint. One teen in the survey registered deep gratitude for a mother who insisted he attend church.

The last thing in the world I wanted to do was go on winter retreat with the church youth group. But my mom told me that I couldn't go

77

out for basketball if I didn't. I was in a bad mood all weekend until Saturday night when the speaker talked to us about Jesus. I gave my life to Christ that night and now nobody could keep me from going to church.—BRYAN, 16

3. Love your pastor and speak well of the church around your teens.

". . . Respect those . . . who are over you in the Lord. . . . Hold them in the highest regard in love . . ." (I Thessalonians 5:12, 13).

The church is an easy target for our criticism because it is made up of fallible human beings. All the sins that plague the world (greed, pride, lust, etc.) petition the church for equal time and usually gain admittance. One hopes that as Christians grow in grace they also will grow in personal holiness, but "sinless bliss" will never describe the church on this side of heaven.

The Christian parent should reserve his criticism for his own sins ("Who are you to judge your neighbor?" James 4:12), and leave the judgment of the saints to the One whose love endures forever ("It is I who judge uprightly," Psalm 75:2).

It is my observation that parents who are critical of the church tend to raise teens who become hyper-critical of it. When speaking of the church and its pastor, the wise Christian parent will heed Paul's exhortation in Ephesians 4:29a, "Do not let any unwholesome talk come out of your mouths, but only what is helpful for building others up according to their needs."

One of the most promising revelations of this study is that, next to the Christian home, the church remains the most effective evangelist of teenagers—just as it was almost 2,000 years ago. Discerning parents with hope for their teens' salvation will support the church not only with their presence and their tithes, but with grateful hearts as well.

CHAPTER
7

Friends Can Be Friends Forever
Evangelizing Your Teen via Friendships

It's no use to cling to rocks that are falling with you.
—ALAN WATTS

A lifetime's not too long to live as friends.
—MICHAEL W. AND DEBBIE SMITH

AFTER POLLING HIGH SCHOOL seniors to answer the question, "What is the one thing which most prevents you from being a Christian?", one religious educator concluded that the major obstacle is fear—"not fear of punishment for their sins, but fear of the pack."[1]

If negative peer influence is one of the major deterrents to adolescent faith decisions, then one might expect that positive Christian peer pressure would be a significant factor for leading teens to faith in Christ. In fact, in my survey, twenty-six percent (278 out of 1,068) of the youth who became Christians during their teenage years named "Christian friends" as the reason for making that decision—ranking friends as the number two cause for a teen's decision to become a Christian.

A friend of mine had just asked me for the fifth time to go to a lock-in at her church. I was into drugs and dabbling with alcohol, but her persistence paid off. I went to her church, found out about Christ and eventually put my trust in Him.—MARK, 18

My best friend and two other guys decided to start a Bible study during our junior year in high school. I asked him if I could come, and he said,

"Sure, Tom, but you'd probably get more out of it if you were a Christian." We talked 'til 2 a.m. that night, and I asked Jesus into my heart.—TOM, 17

Non-Christian teens usually scrutinize their Christian counterparts with vigilance before they decide for Christ.

I was introduced to Christ by a friend of mine. I saw that Jesus was alive to him and not the storybook person I thought He was.—DERRICK, 15

Some good friends invited me to church, and for nine weeks I was clueless. But all the time I was watching them. After I knew that they weren't phony, that they really loved each other and me too, I accepted Christ.—TEDDY, 16

When I saw how much Christ changed my best friend, I got interested.

—AMY, 14

One of the most profound responses came from a teen who needed a friend to point him to Christ.

I don't know Christ. I don't like people getting to know me, so I put up a front. I guess it's a game that I play, but I think I just need a true friend. Not just Jesus, but a human friend.—ALAN, 16

From the early days of the first-century church, Christian teens have been a powerful influence on their non-Christian friends. A moving example of friendship evangelism is engraved on a wall in the quarters of the imperial page boys on Palatine Hill in Rome. It is a crude picture, drawn by a youthful hand, of a teenage boy standing in a worshipful attitude, with his right hand raised high. The object of his adoration is a figure, the body of a man with the head of an ass. Underneath is scrawled, "Alexamenos worships his God."

One of the pages was a believer and unashamed of it. His classmates were maliciously taunting him for his faith. But the young Christian was not to be discouraged. A second inscription, etched just under the derisive one, reads: "ALEXAMENOS IS FAITHFUL!"

It could be that Alexamenos scribbled his own response to the vicious cartoon. But some scholars believe that the rejoinder came from one of his teenage friends who had come to believe in the cause for which he stood.

The Power of a Teenager's Witness

Few factors influence a teen toward Christ like that of a peer who resolutely stands up for his faith. My own son, who had been witnessing without much effect to his best friend, Tommy, taught me this truth one day when I received a phone call from his junior high school principal.

"Hello, Mr. Laurent. I'm glad I caught you at home. I'm afraid I've got some bad news for you. We have to suspend your son from school for a couple of days."

There is no way to explain to someone who has never parented a teenager the vague sense of fear which resides precisely between that portion of your brain responsible for recalling the name of your car insurance company and the one remembering the name of the principal at your teenager's school.

Being the calm, Christian parent that I am, I blurted, "What? You can't do that! I mean, you must have the wrong kid. My son is a good boy."

"Well, he might be, but it's against the rules at our school to fight, and your son just finished a lively one. Please come over immediately and pick him up."

It seems to be an instinct for most Christian parents to think of their own reputation when their children get into trouble, but I can honestly tell you that my reputation as a minister in our little community was not the first thing on my mind as I pulled into the school parking lot. It was the second thing. The first was whether or not he won the fight.

Expecting him to be shuffling toward the car with his head down, I was surprised to find my son running out to meet me with a smile on his face. From the dozens of things I had planned to say to him, all I could manage was a bewildered, "What in the world happened, son?"

With words framed by a bloodied upper lip, he couldn't relate his story fast enough.

"I was sitting in the cafeteria talking to Tommy," he gushed, "when four guys from my class walked up and said, 'Hey, home boys! Are you goin' to the big rock concert in South Bend Friday night?'

" 'Yeah, sure, I guess so,' Tommy told them, so then they asked me, 'What about you, Chris? You comin' with us? We're gonna have some big-time fun.' "

"The group they were going to hear was bad news, Dad, with some deep satanic connections, so I said, 'No thanks, guys. I think I'll skip this one.'

" 'What's the matter, Chris?' they said. 'Don't you like rock music?'

"I knew right then, Dad, that if I answered truthfully I wouldn't win any popularity contests at school. I was so tempted just to say something like, 'Sure I like it. I've got other things going on Friday night, that's all.' I know they would have left me alone if I had, but I could tell that Tommy was watching me. So my brain shut down and my heart took over.

" 'If you guys want to know the truth, 'Twisted Sister' is not my idea of music.

" 'Oh, yeah? What's your idea of music? 'Mary Had a Little Lamb'?'

"Because they had me so badly outnumbered, Dad, I normally would have just walked away. But I'd just been talking to Tommy about coming to church, and I knew if I backed down from those guys, he would think Christianity was for wimps. So I just told them what I believed.

" 'Yeah, that's a pretty good song. But my favorite groups are Petra, Whiteheart, Michael W. Smith, and Carman. If you haven't heard of them, it's because they're Christian bands.' That did it! I knew as soon as the words left my mouth that those guys would never let up on me, but it felt good to say them in front of Tommy.

" 'Christian bands!' they howled, loud enough for everyone in the cafeteria to hear. 'Hey, choirboy! We know what your favorite song is, 'Jesus Loves Me, This I Know'!'

"You know somethin', Dad? I think for the first time in my life I knew that I really believed all of it. Something hardened inside me, and I was glad Tommy was there. They probably weren't expecting a reply, but I looked up and said, 'Yeah, I like that song a lot!'

" 'All right, then, let's sing it for Mr. Christianity, guys.'

"I know they were mocking me out, but I couldn't help but think, I'll bet this is the first time students have ever sung 'Jesus Loves Me' out loud in the school cafeteria. I probably shouldn't have, but I smiled and said 'Thanks, guys. That was beautiful.' Then I turned to Tommy. 'C'mon, let's go to homeroom. It's almost time for the bell to ring.'

"They were standing so that I had to walk right through the middle of them to get to class. When I approached, the biggest guy in the group grabbed me and said, 'Mr. Christianity doesn't like our music, guys.' Then he threw me hard into the lockers against the wall. I remember you told me, Dad, that if someone slaps you on one cheek, you're supposed to let him do it again. So I let him slam me against the lockers a second time. But I don't remember you ever teaching me that Jesus said I had to let him do it three times, so when he went to grab me again, 'Mr. Christianity' punched him in the nose and knocked him down. That's when the principal came and broke things up."

At this point, the average parent would question his teen as to just how much trouble he was now in. Just how severe was this suspension? But not me; I'm more mature. I said, "So, you knocked that bully right on his behind, huh?"

"Yeah, Dad, but that's not important. The great thing is that Tommy told me later he wants to start coming to church with me!"

Charlie Riggs of the Billy Graham Team reports that twenty years ago, most of the teenagers who were making decisions at Graham crusades were from "the liberal churches where they were not hearing the Gospel." But now he observes that more than ninety percent of those making decisions are from our evangelical churches.

If more than ninety percent of teenage evangelism is being done among the youth who are already members of our Gospel-preaching churches, we have a major communication gap with the unchurched teen.[2] Never has friendship evangelism been more important than it is today. It is a fact that no one can reach a non-Christian teen like a believing friend.

Soon after a friend of mine at school helped me become a Christian, I started taking my Bible to study hall. But the study hall teacher said that it was against the law for me to read it at school. So my friend and I started sneaking it in and reading it when the teacher wasn't paying any attention to us. Tons of kids heard about how they wouldn't let us read our Bibles, so some of them started bringing theirs too. So far, we've helped five more students become Christians.—BILL, 16

Some churches are moving in the direction of encouraging their youth to establish "intentional Christian friendships" with the lost teenagers in their schools. Pastor and author Gene Getz instructed his congregation that one visit to the church building in a week was enough. He believes that more than that would steal from them the prime time they need with their non-Christian friends.

We need Christian teens, as Joe Aldrich says, "who are being urged to go out and mix it up at the front lines . . . with the non-Christian community. We need to deploy Christians into the world."[3] The unchurched teen will not come to us. Christian teens must reach them on their own turf.

WHY NON-CHRISTIAN TEENS ARE READY FOR CONVERSION

That teens are in crisis today is well-documented. A 1990 joint commission of educators and the American Medical Association report these alarming statistics: "One million teens get pregnant each year, fifty percent of high school seniors get drunk once a month, and more than 500,000 teens run away or are homeless each year."[4]

But problems like these are only symptomatic of a deeper crisis. Most teens are faced with three choices on almost a daily basis, and whichever choice they make is likely to drive them to despair and/or aberrant behavior.

First, when confronted by conflicting pressures from peers and parents, they can turn off their peers and devote themselves totally to satisfying the important adults and authority figures in their lives. Such a teenager often develops into either an obsequious, fawning child with no backbone or an inwardly angry teen with a growing bitterness toward his parents which puts the two sides on an ugly collision course. Parents who encourage their teens to choose this course are either sub-human or plain ignorant.

Second, a teenager can reject the adult establishment and, for better or worse, choose to go all the way with the peer group. This teen usually shows early signs of destructive behavior and often is never restored to the family circle.

The third choice is the one most often made by teenagers: to compromise and try to please everyone. Such teens feel obliged to live up to roles imposed by parents, teachers, peers, and just about everyone in between. To keep conflict at a minimum, they will talk one way to their parents, another to their teachers, and a third to their peers—even about the same subjects. Juggling these roles and switching masks with environments will inevitably lead the teen to identity confusion and serious questions like, "Who is the real me?" or "How am I going to find out who I really am?" Such teens are crying out for a sense of purpose and belonging. They are prime candidates for some type of conversion experience.

It is at this critical time of self-doubt that teenagers are most vulnerable to outside influence, Christian or non-Christian. I am of the opinion that whichever side establishes the strongest friendship with such teens will win them over for years, perhaps forever.

HOW TO WIN A TEENAGER TO CHRIST

When researchers ask teenagers whether or not they believe in God, the high numbers who respond positively (almost ninety-five percent) can lead us to assume that there is much Christian commitment among contemporary teens. Rinus Baljeu of The Navigators decided to correct this misconception by asking the teens in his study to respond to the statement, "I think the following could give my life more meaning. . . ."

Eighty-seven percent of the teens thought that meaning could be found in a good job, eighty-five percent voted for finding meaning in a marriage partner, and eighty-four percent believed that they could find more meaning in life through sports and recreation. Bringing up the rear were the fifteen percent who thought that quiet time and prayer could help, which exactly tied the number of teens who concluded that alcohol and drugs could help them find meaning.

About eighty percent of the teens he surveyed considered the question of the meaning of life important while that same number (eighty percent) deemed it unimportant whether Jesus Christ existed as a man on earth or not. Eighty-five percent reckoned it unimportant whether Jesus is the Son of God or not, and a full seventy-five percent considered the question of God's existence to be unimportant!

Jim Petersen claims that even though teens are concerned about the meaning of life, they are giving up on "traditional religious explanations."[5] They are basically unconcerned about the existence of God. Only immediate concerns like girlfriends, boyfriends, and jobs are important to them. So when evangelizing teenagers, according to Petersen, "relationships are of primary concern."[6]

Propositional truths carry little weight with a teen until a friendship has been developed. Dann Spader reminds us that "secular educators have demonstrated that children twelve years and younger are primarily influenced by rewards and punishments, while mature adults are motivated through cognitive thinking and stimulating ideas. But teens determine what's true based on what they experience in relationships."[7]

Therefore, if you want to win teenagers to Christ, you must build a loving relationship with them. One of the teens in my survey wrote of the lasting impact that friendships can have on faith.

I went to church camp as a favor to my dad. He was always on my back about God loving me, etc. It seems like everybody's had some sort of pseudo-renewal experience at "Some Camp, U.S.A.," and I was determined not to be the next in line. But . . . I met Christians there. Whether they were Christians just for the week or what—they were good to me, and cared about me even when they knew I was different. I had had intentions of blowing the whole thing off—I'd brought cigarettes, etc.—thinking there'd be other "rebels" there who would be willing to break the rules. I guess that knowing that people cared about me made me see life and God differently. Just love me first, then love me to Christ!—MARK, 18

But what about teens who do not have intimate Christian peers to influence them? Enter the Christian parents, often feeling like losers in the struggles with the non-Christian peers of their sons and daughters. They must remember one thing: although peers are more likely to influence immediate behavior, parents have a much greater influence over permanent values. Adolescents are easily pressured to go along with the crowd, but this occurs in the area of action rather than in fundamental attitudes. In this domain, parents still carry significant weight. Now consider some biblical advice for influencing your teens in both areas.

WHAT'S A PARENT TO DO?

1. You can still be your teen's "best friend."

"There are 'friends' who pretend to be friends, but there is a friend who sticks closer than a brother" (Proverbs 18:24, TLB).

Myron Brenton writes in *How to Survive Your Child's Rebellious Teens*, "Friends considered poor influences offer excitement—a lightning rod for the electric crackle of anger the rebellious child so strongly feels inside himself. More than that, they offer acceptance and intimacy."[8]

Recently two Texas researchers, Spyros Catechis and Joe Carbonari, observed fifty families with teens ranging from sixteen to eighteen. Half of the children were labeled delinquent because of behavior which landed them in a court-appointed treatment setting. The other half of the teens were selected from reasonably tranquil homes in suburban Houston. Catechis and Carbonari discovered some critical differences in the way the two kinds of families functioned.

- The delinquent teens—unlike the others—reported a large amount of inconsistency in the way their parents communicated with them.
- The delinquent ones—unlike the well-adjusted teens—perceived the same kind of inconsistency in the way their mothers and fathers related to each other.
- In the families of the delinquent teens, the parents had a great deal of trouble expressing their feelings—feelings of vulnerability as well as positive feelings. A sense of closeness was missing, and the delinquent teens said that they definitely felt this lack.

When teenagers who consistently get into trouble are asked what they receive from those friends to whom their parents object so much, their frequent answer is. "They accept me and they love me." My wife and I resolved years ago to make sure that our teenagers would never have reason to doubt our love or acceptance. Our seventeen-year-old son saved one of the many letters that we wrote to him during his summer mission trip to Scotland.

> We miss you, buddy. Proud is not a strong enough word for how all of us feel about you. No family in this solar system has a better son. Your love for Jesus and love for others (especially those less fortunate) has always been a great inspiration to us. You've heard us say it before, but it's still true: We're some of the only parents we know whose greatest hero is their son.

Because we encourage our teens to go into the world with their faith, and we kick them out of the nest as often as possible to do so, we have little fear that our undying love for them will inflate their egos or encourage them to be self-consumed. The world has a poor track record for its acceptance of Christian teens.

"In this world you will have trouble," says Jesus to my teenagers (John 16:33). One thing we Christian parents can count on is that our children will receive pride-shattering blows from a world that hates them, because we have raised them as Christians and they do not belong to it (John 15:19). If my children want temporary love, destructive criticism, and contemptuous regard, they can go to the world. If they want unconditional love, they can come to their parents.

I have never met any teenagers who would not gladly accept a loving parent as one of their best friends. Such parents will have a major impact on the decision that their teens make about Christ.

2. *If you need to ask your teen's forgiveness, do it now while there is still time.*

"First go and be reconciled to your [teen]; then come and offer your gift [to God]" (Matthew 5:24).

Saying "I'm sorry" is not second nature to most parents, but by the time your children become teenagers, they have learned firsthand that you are fallible. The parent who is unable to admit faults will only further alienate the teenager who could be won over by an honest confession.

I spoke recently with a teenager whose father was unwittingly driving her away from Christianity by his overprotectiveness and legalistic spirit.

"It's hard to live with a 'perfect' father, or at least one who thinks he is," she told me. "As far as I can remember, he has never apologized to me for anything. Yet I've heard him lie to my friends on the phone by telling them that I wasn't home. I have to hide all my letters because I know he goes through my dresser drawers looking for them. He even walks past my Sunday school class just to check and see whether or not I've skipped out. People might see us as a Christian family, but living at home is hell for me."

I asked her for permission to speak with her father. When we met, I strongly advised him to change his dictatorial approach. His instinct was to be defensive.

"Nobody loves Jennifer more than I do. Would you rather I didn't care so much about her?"

"No one is doubting your concern for your daughter," I replied. "I really believe that your highest goal is for her to grow into a strong Christian woman. But your controlling methods are not accomplishing that goal." I warned him that I sincerely felt he was influencing his daughter, at that critical "faith crisis" time most teens experience, to decide against Christianity.

At first he seemed shocked, then humbled. His last intention was to provoke his daughter away from the faith. When he asked me for advice, I pointed him to James 5:16 ("Admit your faults to one another . . . so that you may be healed", TLB) and suggested that, for starters, he should apologize to his sixteen year old.

Teenagers are resilient and make good forgivers . . . if the parent doesn't wait too long. Joyce Vedral cautions parents not to put off asking their teens to forgive them.

" 'Why should I go to all this trouble?' you may ask. You should do it because every undealt-with hurt serves to permanently widen the rift between the parent and the teen—and that rift can eventually result in much more than a communication gap. It can end up becoming a gulf that separates so many adults from their parents— for life. It's much easier to express our sincere apologies now, when they can do the most good, than to wait until years later, when things have crystallized into permanent resentment."[9]

3. *Pray daily for God to bring at least one solid Christian friend into your teen's life.*

"Though one may be overpowered, two can defend themselves" (Ecclesiastes 4:12).

Several years ago psychologists designed an interesting experiment to study peer pressure. One hundred groups of seven teenagers each were presented the following two cards to analyze.

Each group was then asked, "Which line in the box on the right is the same length as the line in the box on the left?" The answer is, of course, #2, but before the experiment began, six of the teens were told to answer #1. Although #2 is clearly the correct answer, the hypothesis was that most teenagers would agree with the majority vote. The results of the experiment revealed that over seventy-five percent of the teens who were tested did exactly that.

When asked about it later, most confessed they had used some type of excuse to talk themselves into going along with the crowd. "Maybe I don't understand the instructions," some thought. Others decided that something must be wrong with their vision. The few who resisted the peer influence and voted against the group reported a lot of discomfort and didn't like being different.

Then the researchers gave a hundred different groups the same test. This time, they instructed one of the six to answer #2. When the teens being tested had just one vote to agree with them, only twenty-five percent went along with the incorrect majority.[10]

It is a fact that teens who have at least one intimate Christian friend can resist negative peer influence far better than those who have none.

4. Make peace with your teenagers' friends.

"I have become all things to all men so that by all possible means I might save some" (I Corinthians 9:22b).

It seems to be a fact of human nature that the moment you express your dislike or distrust for one of your teenager's friends, your child will likely declare undying loyalty to that person. The moment you order your teen to stop seeing a particular friend, you can expect either a blatant, angry refusal or, which might be worse, a sullen "all right"—a promise they have no intention of keeping.

Teens meet forbidden friends on the sly all the time. Paul Borthwick writes, "Parental disapproval of an undesirable friend almost always ensures the fact that the teen will cling to that friend. The desire in a teenager to be independent from parents makes him take parental disapproval as a 'dare' regarding a bad-influence peer."[11]

Christian parents would be wiser to be as accepting as possible of their teens' friends. Such acceptance defuses your teenagers' need to shock you with a negative choice and might influence them to choose more edifying friends.

Furthermore, the Christian parent might be the one who is able to lead their teen's friend to a life-giving relationship with Jesus

Christ. Because my teenagers have several non-Christian friends from public high school, and the front doors of our home and refrigerator are open to them, I have had many wonderful opportunities to talk with them about God's love. In the most natural atmosphere of all, the easy give-and-take of a Christian family setting, our teens' friends can be remarkably moved toward Christianity.

5. *When the time is right, encourage your own teens to share the Good News with their non-Christian friends.*

"Give and it will be given to you" (Luke 6:38a).

It is a spiritual truth that the more you give away your faith, the more faith you will have to give. I have seen my own teens grow more as Christians when they are evangelizing their friends than at any other time. Some teenagers seem to have a strong sense of responsibility for sharing their faith. Others could use a gentle reminder now and then from their parents—or, even better, a living example.

This study has confirmed that, next to the church as evangelist, no one shares Christ with teens better than their Christian friends. Parents who remember that friends really can be "friends forever" will make evangelism a priority in the home.

CHAPTER
8

The Youth Pastor as Evangelist

The world cannot hate us, we are too much like its own. Oh, that God would make us dangerous!—JIM ELLIOTT

"I CAN'T BELIEVE IT!" LAMENTED Todd, a youth pastor friend of mine. "Do you know what the youth committee at my church are going to do? They want to cut me back to half time to 'balance the church budget.' Eight months ago they said they wanted a great youth program, and now they want twice as much for half the price. I've worked harder than I ever have in my life—weekends, nights, holidays—and they all know it. But they don't think they're getting enough for the paltry $13,000 they pay me. Can you believe it?"

I continued listening to the outpouring of his frustration, dispirited words frequently voiced by beleaguered youth pastors.

"Half of the people at our church want a baby-sitter, others want an evangelical Mother Goose, some don't understand why the associate pastor can't do the job, the senior pastor doesn't seem to care as long as he doesn't have the teenagers bothering him, and the kids could care less as long as they have a good time. Is it all worth it?"

Most of my heroes are youth pastors. I've always championed the underdog, and the typical youth pastor is a classic example. Their job description is never-ending. We expect them to be able to counsel our teens with the insight of trained psychologists, communicate ancient truths with the flair of gifted preachers, administer their program with the competence of seasoned corporate executives—and then we pay them like baby-sitters, which is the one task they would have thoroughly rejected had they known it would be a part of their job description.

I supervise the youth ministry program at the college where I teach. One of the first things I tell my students is not to enter our program unless they are prepared for a position characterized by bad hours, low pay, difficult parents, moody teens, a surplus of criticism from the church—and more joy than any human being has a right to experience. Material compensations may be minimal for the youth pastor, but the spiritual rewards can be phenomenal.

Actually, I have more compassion for senior pastors, because the bulk of their ministry is done among us adults, known for our rigidity and spiritual complacency. Teenagers, on the other hand, are still people-in-transition, eager for a conversion experience and ardent for Christ when their faith takes root. Youth pastors may be the most selfless, underappreciated, overworked, and underpaid laborers in the Church today, but they are ministering in the most fertile arena of all for making a spiritual impact on lives.

Christian parents will not find a more capable ally for moving their teens toward Jesus Christ. In this study, twenty-three percent (263 out of 1,068) of the youth who decided for Christ during their teenage years named "youth pastor" as the reason for making that commitment—ranking it just after "church" and "Christian friends."

I met our youth pastor on a church retreat. He sat and talked with me for four hours. I can honestly say that if it wasn't for him, I'd never have become a Christian. Teenagers need someone to really talk to and accept them—also to understand them.—DAVE, 16

I became a Christian because of the integrity that I saw in the little things in my youth leader's life—like following the speed limit, being morally pure in his dating life, and the way he would go out of his way to help others.—JASON, 15

More than one youth pastor has filled in as a surrogate parent for those who have abandoned their teens.

My dad was a drug dealer, my mother an alcoholic, and I knew that was how I was going to be. But I guess God was watching over me, because when my parents took off to Florida to run away from their debts, our youth pastor and his wife took me and my sister in to live with them. They led me to Christ, and now I'm not one bit ashamed to tell of my past experiences because these things have made me a better person and a strong Christian. My parents aren't Christians yet, but they are "straight" and I praise God for them and what He's brought me through!—MARCIA, 16

PERSONALIZING THE GOSPEL

When God wanted to reach us, He did not schedule a meeting and invite us to attend. He "became flesh and dwelt among us" (John 1:14, RSV). In the same way, a youth program alone will not change a teen's life. The Gospel must be personalized, and few have the opportunity to do that better than the youth pastor.

Youth counselor Ben Mijuskovic claims that teens are "animated by a fear of loneliness."[1] He believes that the drive to escape isolation accounts for all of a teen's passion, thought, and action. The causes of loneliness among teens are many: anxiety over the visible changes in their bodies, separation from parents, an increasing and frightening sense of autonomy, the struggle for meaning, feelings of rejection, changing family structures, poor parent-teen relationships, etc.—and that is the normal adolescent!

But according to most psychologists, there is a remedy: a meaningful relationship with an individual who loves them. The universal problem of loneliness among teens can be overcome when a mutual relationship of trust, respect, and Christian love exists between the teen and another person. For many Christian teens today, that person is their youth pastor.

I came to know Christ through our youth pastor. He showed me so much love and how to have fun as a Christian. He was always there for me even after he moved to Canada. I know that I have failed in my Christian walk many times but whenever I think about my youth pastor, I get excited again and feel loved.—GAIL, 17

Christian parents need youth pastors and other youth leaders even more than they realize. At a time in life when adolescents are naturally separating from their parents, youth pastors can step in and provide spiritual guidance acceptable to the teens and in accord with the moral and religious values of their families. As both a Christian parent of teens and an adolescent psychologist, I have some practical advice for all youth pastors and leaders.

GOALS FOR OUR YOUTH PASTORS

1. Offer our teens what the world cannot give them.

"So from now on we regard no [teen] from a worldly point of view" (II Corinthians 5:16a).

I have always had a tendency to believe that in order to keep teenagers' attention, we have to entertain them into the kingdom of God. Jesus would have had real problems with me if I had been one of the twelve. I can hear Him gently rebuking me, "Bob, the fish and the loaves are enough. We don't need to pass out free water pouches just to hold this crowd." Or, "Forget the camel race idea, Bob. I'm going to preach the Sermon on the Mount instead."

Diligent preparation, innovative programming, and creative planning can all be used by the Holy Spirit to affect teens. But the trouble with entertaining teens to reach them for Christ is that when the show is over, their shallow commitment fades quickly. If the focus of their ministry is on ensuring attendance through entertainment, youth pastors must be prepared to witness the dissipation of their programs when the novel ideas begin to dwindle.

In my efforts to compete with the world for the teens' attention, there have been times when I've been guilty of using the world's methods and missing out on that singular strategy God has always used to call teenagers to His Son. It is the one method that reaches teens and keeps them faithful better than any other, and I rediscovered it a few years ago at an unusual youth retreat.

A youth pastor friend invited me to speak at his retreat and promised me an extraordinary encounter with God. When he said, "Just bring a sleeping bag and a change of clothes; you won't need any meal money," I assumed he meant that he would take care of my food expenses. As it turned out, there were no expenses because there was no food—for the entire weekend!

When he met me at the camp, he rehearsed the three-day schedule with me. I remember saying something spiritual, like "You mean there won't be a single meal? I can't even eat this apple I brought?" He told me that instead of meals, we would be having Bible studies at that time. The hundred-plus teens would be donating the money they would have spent on meals to a fund to feed the homeless in Chicago.

It was the first time I had ever fasted for more than a day, and I could hardly believe that these teenagers had agreed to it. "On the contrary," he informed me, "It was their idea. They're excited about it."

"But what are you going to do about recreation? And what band did you hire to come in and do an evening concert?" I asked with a measure of foreboding.

"Instead of playing games, we're going to have training sessions in practical evangelism so that when we go back to school on Monday, we'll be prepared to share our faith with our lost friends. And instead of the usual Saturday evening rock concert, we're going to kick off a fantastic concert of prayer." As if he could read my mind, he added, "And just in case you're wondering, all of the teens are—"

"I know, I know," I broke in, laughing. "They're all really excited about it."

It was, without exception, the finest youth retreat I've ever experienced. The very austerity and simplicity of the weekend was a major part of its appeal to the youth. The youth pastor related to me later that the teens at the retreat grew more in one weekend of mutual self-denial and radical commitment than they had during his entire two-year tenure at their church. Their light but meaningful suffering had bonded the youth group together in a way they had never experienced before. I asked my friend how he had struck upon this idea.

He explained, "I was getting tired of trying to keep my teens pumped up all the time with one high after another—amusement parks, Christian rock concerts, beach parties, hay rides, etc. Then one day I read Jesus' words, 'If anyone comes to me and does not hate . . . even his own life—he cannot be my disciple. And anyone who does not carry his cross and follow me cannot be my disciple. . . . In the same way, any of you who does not give up everything he has cannot be my disciple' (Luke 14:26-27, 33).

"I had to ask myself the question, 'Are my methods actually keeping my teens from becoming true disciples?' It occurred to me that I had been going about youth ministry in the wrong way. Maybe I had been asking too little of the kids. I knew that it was time to try Jesus' strategy."

This youth pastor has learned the real key to reaching teens for Christ. They will not respond to a faith that is for the timid, the unthinking, or the ossified. Teenagers thrive on being dared to do the extraordinary for God. They can be won back by the two-fisted challenge of the rugged God-man who defies easy believism among teens with His words: "I know you well—you are neither hot nor cold; I wish you were one or the other. But since you are merely lukewarm, I will spit you out of my mouth!" (Revelation 3:15, 16, TLB).

The type of religion which strikes at the very center of the teenage ethos is real Christianity: muscular and demanding. It calls for banners and trumpets and drums and battle gear and all the strength a teen can give it, not soft words and hesitant manners and mild preaching. It demands a "Yes!" to the face of God, regardless of persecution or even death, and a joyful noise before the Lord.

Jim Elliott punctures our spiritual complacency with words which, thirty years after he spoke them, still pierce like cold steel:

> We are so utterly ordinary, so commonplace, while we profess to know a power the 20th Century does not reckon with. But we are "harmless," and therefore unharmed. We are spiritual pacifists, non-militants, conscientious objectors in this battle-to-the-death with principalities and powers in high places. Meekness must be had for contact with men, but brass, outspoken boldness is required to take part in the comradeship of the Cross. We are 'sideliners'—coaching and criticizing the real wrestlers while content to sit by and leave the enemies of God unchallenged. The world cannot hate us, we are too much like its own. Oh that God would make us dangerous![2]

2. Bring our teens to a sense of mission.

"Whatever you did for one of the least of these brothers of mine, you did for me" (Matthew 25:40).

"If there was ever a generation concerned with itself, it is today's youth," concludes a recent University of Michigan study. "The teen of today is more interested in making money than anything else; all social service organizations have grown less attractive to them."[3]

Christopher Lasch, author of *The Culture of Narcissism*, describes the contemporary adolescent as being "absorbed in his own private performance." He writes, "To live for the moment is his prevailing passion—to live for himself, not for his predecessors or posterity."[4]

It is the youth pastor's unique position to minimize adolescent egocentrism by calling teens to a Cause that is greater than the self, and in so doing, to reach them permanently for Christ. Teenagers learn by doing and need a ministry of participation before they can make the Christian faith their own.

"One of the reasons for the increased arguing and tension between teens and their parents," claims developmental psychologist Lawrence Kutner, "is that our culture does not have a clear rite of passage which quickly defines the beginning of adulthood."[5] Unwittingly we spend the years from the time our children reach sexual maturity to the time they live independently giving them mixed messages regarding their roles and status.

I encourage the church today to resurrect a tradition prevalent not only in the homes and synagogues of Old Testament times but integral to the family unit in the early New Testament church: the bar mitzvah ("son of the commandment") experience. When a boy reached thirteen years of age, he was given the full rights and religious responsibilities of an adult. This same level of respect should at least be approached for our own teenagers now.

We have spiritually disenfranchised our children at precisely the time they desperately need to be included, disempowering them just when we demand they become more responsible. The teens in my study responded "strongly agree" to the following two statements, "God could never use me to do anything," and "If anyone in my church ever asked me to do anything important, I'd be shocked."

Howard Burbach found that teens "who fail to become involved in church activities may either be alienated or in a high-risk category. Whereas research has shown that adolescents who are involved in service-related activities have far lower levels of alienation."[6]

The youth pastor must proclaim Christian causes and call for teens to work for those causes. Many teens make an irreversible decision for Christ when they are used by God to serve others. George Hunter relates a wonderful story about a girl who gave her life to Christ after joining in the civil rights movement.

"She and her roommate decided to join Martin Luther King and his people in the now historic march from Selma to Montgomery. During the first day and a half of that march she felt something very strange and awesome and wonderful happening within her. It seemed as though she was in touch with Something that she had never been in touch with before. She mustered the courage to approach Dr. King and asked him what was happening to her. He replied, 'I cannot be sure, but I believe that in your service to Him, Christ is making His approach to you. 'Inasmuch as ye have done it unto one of the least of these my brethren,' quoted Dr. King, 'ye have done it unto me.' Soon after, she made a conscious decision to give her life over to the Lord Jesus Christ."[7]

When we enlist teenagers in the ministry of the church, evangelism becomes the handmaid to mission. There are great Christian causes to which teens can give their lives, causes that are of the essence of the kingdom of God, and often in surrendering to the cause, a teenager finds the One who is behind it all.

3. Encourage our teens to confront the world with their faith.

"Don't let anyone look down on you because you are young, but set an example for the believers in speech, in life, in love, in faith and in purity. . . . Persevere in them, because if you do, you will save both yourself and your hearers" (I Timothy 4:12, 16).

Recently I read a remarkable statement from a well-known Christian author. He said that if we did not prepare our teenagers for their encounters with non-Christians in the world, then perhaps isolation would be our best strategy! Of course I understand the author's rationale for that statement; we are losing too many Christian teens to the secular world. But isolation is neither biblical nor possible.

As Christian parents who fear the world's impact on our teens, we are tempted to build up walls of thought and Christian exclusivism. Instead of passing along to our teenagers a faith that can overcome evil with good, we are often guilty of merely teaching them how to retreat from the battle. Instead of equipping them to fight the good fight of faith, we have tried to insulate them from it. Such a withdrawal can have devastating effects on a teenager's faith.

One of the results of withdrawing from the world (not to be confused with withdrawing from sin) is a terrible sense of boredom and frustration. Life becomes pale and uninteresting, and at this point church, for many teens, becomes "business as usual." When going to church becomes a routine to be played out, when there is little that is challenging, gripping, fascinating, or exciting about their faith, teenagers are not far from leaving it behind.

Youth pastors must encourage teens to know the exhilaration of taking their faith into the world and discovering that "greater is he that is in you, than he that is in the world" (I John 4:4, KJV). The apostle Paul issues a battle cry to today's teen: "Do everything without complaining or arguing, so that you may become blameless and pure, children of God without fault in a crooked and depraved generation, in which you shine like stars in the universe as you hold out the word of life" (Philippians 2:14-16a).

Not only is it unbiblical for us to advise our teens to isolate themselves from the world, it is well-nigh impossible. With the advent of cable television, the increasing secularization of public schools, and the constant pressure from non-Christian friends, church-related teens are very much a part of the world. The youth pastor's main focus then should be to help our teens to live with intentionality as Christians in a non-Christian environment.

God's purpose for sending teenagers into the world is not simply because their lost friends need a Christian witness, but because He knows that the aggressive positioning of teens in the world for the purpose of confronting it with His love will keep their faith fresh and new. When teens lose sight of their call to represent Him in their daily life away from home, not only does their faith fade quickly, but the world usually claims them for its own.

It is precisely this constant threat of being overtaken by the world which sustains the vitality of teens' faith and rivets their attention on the present mission. When my son returned home from his summer mission trip to Scotland and faced parents eager for a debriefing session, he calmly recited much of his schedule in a perfunctory manner. But when he told of his ministry among the street gangs of Glasgow, his eyes flashed with excitement and the intensity of his voice betrayed a new passion in his faith.

Peter Marshall once observed, "Today's Christians are like deep-sea divers, incased in suits designed for fathoms deep, marching bravely forth to pull plugs out of bathtubs."[8] God created teenagers with a desire to dare. The wise youth pastor knows that they will not be satisfied with bathtub diving . . . they want to plunge into the sea.

WHAT'S A PARENT TO DO?

There are several things that concerned Christian parents can do to help their teens come to Christ through the influence of a youth pastor.

1. If your local church does not have a youth pastor on its ministry team, encourage them to employ one.

One pastor polled the teenagers in his own congregation who were present at most of the youth group meetings and found that two-thirds of them felt coerced by their parents into attendance. That pastor believes that typical church-related teens are "much more interested in each other and the wall clock" than they are in the content of the youth program. He fears that his church is very representative of most mainline congregations: "fifteen to twenty-five bored teens in a church with over 300 families."[9]

What can be done about this spiritual malaise among our youth? Opening the church pocketbook to enlist the help of a youth pastor is a start in the right direction. Dennis Miller, president of Church Youth Development, asks, "Who can students turn to for help and answers to these complex and dangerous issues? Teenagers desperately need youth pastors who care and know that a personal relationship with God is the first and most important step in finding answers."

Miller reports that "the church has a great lack of clergy working with youth. In fact, only 2.8 percent of the total clergy minister to youth."[10] Churches simply must do better in this area. One denominational executive reports that ninety-two percent of the students without a youth pastor who graduate from their youth groups "fail to continue a life of commitment to God or to the church within eighteen months of graduation."[11]

2. Help your church get its priorities straight when looking for a youth pastor.

I tell my students that there are actually only three qualifications for being a good youth pastor. You must be someone who truly loves teens, who has demonstrated moral integrity, and who will point the children to Jesus Christ. If our youth pastors possess these qualities, they should be quickly forgiven for others they may lack.

I have known scores of churches who have been burned by prioritizing the wrong assets. It matters little that candidates are clever and quick-witted if they care more for themselves than the teens they are ordained to serve. To choose a youth pastor because of physical attractiveness, musical ability, or athletic ability is a poor trade-off if the youth program is scandalized by the leader's lack of sexual restraint. Educational credentials are worthless if the choice as youth pastor is neither Christ-centered nor rooted in the Scriptures.

3. Give your youth pastor a clear job description and the authority to carry it out.

It is not unusual to see a church advertise for someone to fill the following impossible position: "Youth minister/Director of Christian Education: suburban church seeks dedicated pastor to direct comprehensive youth program—educational, spiritual, social opportunity to administer established primary-grade program and to develop a promising teenage ministry. Send resume. . . ."

I know of no one in this part of the solar system without a red "S" on his chest who could fulfill such a job description, and yet, youth pastors commonly face such unrealistic expectations. It is enough that they bring your teens to Christ and help keep them there.

More than ever, churches are recognizing the crucial need to evangelize teenagers. Dann Spader announces, "We no longer can be content with just Christian nurture in our youth programming. We must aggressively seek to reach and win young people to the person of Jesus Christ."[12] Few are positioned for this task better than the youth pastor.

CHAPTER
9

Communicating Christ Through a Crisis

A certain amount of opposition is a great help for a man. Kites rise against and not with the wind.
—JOHN NEAL

Godly sorrow brings repentance that leads to salvation.
—THE APOSTLE PAUL

WE RAISED GINGER FROM A puppy, and she was the most beautiful Irish setter I'd ever seen. I'm not certain if anyone knows just when an animal becomes a bonafide member of the family, but this shaggy-haired, auburn charmer wagged her way into our hearts early on. Countless times as I was leaving my loved ones to go on a speaking trip, I would take one last wistful look up the driveway, only to see Ginger playfully wrestling with my son under the maple tree. Somehow I knew things would be all right under the watchful eye of that great canine sentry.

Whenever I returned home late at night, my wife and children soundly sleeping, I knew as I stepped from the car that I would be greeted by that setter tail rapping out its welcome against the side of the garage. Interrupting her constant vigil over our home, I stroked her furry coat and knew that she was one of us. We could never have been prepared for the rainy Saturday morning when she was struck by a panel truck one block from our house. We buried her in a muddy grave behind her doghouse, and a part of each one of us died with her.

C. S. Lewis said, "God whispers in our pleasure, but He shouts in our pain." His consoling voice was loud and clear that day, "O, Death where is your sting; O, grave where then your victory?" as my young family and I stood in a steady downpour, embracing, weeping, and growing together as we never had before.

As I consider it now, I cannot think of a time when God did something wonderful in my family without starting with something very difficult. It seems to be a fact of human nature that we need to be pushed to our extremity before we cry out to Him for salvation. "The Lord is close to the brokenhearted," sings King David, "and saves those who are crushed in spirit" (Psalm 34:18).

I was not surprised to find in this study that, although God is never the architect of their suffering, He often uses painful crises to lead teenagers to a saving knowledge of His Son. A full eleven percent (117 out of 1,068) of the students who decided for Christ after they reached their teenage years cited "suffering/crisis" as the reason they made that commitment.

During my junior year in high school, I was in an almost-fatal car accident. A friend from church came to the hospital and shared the plan of salvation with me. If God hadn't gotten me flat on my back, I probably never would have become a Christian.—ROBERT, 17

After my boyfriend and I broke up, I was totally devastated. I turned to alcohol, drugs, and sex and went through a year and a half of total hell on earth. When I got as low as anybody could get, I knew that I needed help. A Christian guy at work named Mike saw my hurt and knew that I needed Jesus.—MARGARET, 18

On June 1st at 2:00 a.m., I hit a tree on my motorcycle going ninety miles per hour. For six hours in the emergency room, I had time to think about my life. Both God's anger and love that my mom and grandma had talked to me about before seemed suddenly very real. I knew that I had to make a choice. My new life started there in Sherman Hospital with a broken body and a broken heart.—DAVID, 16

FROM SUFFERING TO SALVATION

St. Louis psychologist Kathryn Cramer is an expert on stress and suffering. She describes how teens might come to Christ through four stages after a crisis: challenge, exploration, invention, and transformation.

In stage one, *challenge,* teens are simply trying to get through the shock of the crisis. Most of them will experience a combination of fear, anger, and disorientation. The major coping asset in this stage is *courage*. Instead of encouraging our teens to flee from the problem, "either by physically escaping it or psychologically denying it," Cramer believes that parents should advise them to view the trauma as an opportunity for growth and possibly spiritual salvation.

By stage two, *exploration*, teens are in a better position to evaluate the impact of the crisis. Through the major coping asset of *curiosity* and with the help of Christian friends or family members, they can receive hope that something good can happen out of the crisis.

In stage three, *invention*, Christian parents or concerned friends are able, through the coping asset—*creativity*—to help teens-in-crisis see the possibility of being restored both spiritually and emotionally. During this stage, confidantes should not be tentative about pointing teens to the sufficiency of Jesus Christ.

Finally, in stage four, *transformation*, a decision for Christ brings satisfaction, meaning, and growth from the original crisis. Through *commitment*—this stage's major coping asset—the teen continues to be open to new areas of spiritual maturation made possible through trauma.[1]

The fact is that it often takes a crisis to get our attention. I can think of few experiences more mundane than the Friday afternoon flight from Chicago to Des Moines. The plane is usually filled with beleaguered businessmen anxious to get home for the weekend, and the inattention they pay to the flight attendant's instructions is absolute. I always feel sorry for the attendant, persevering through a mechanical presentation to a cabin of indifferent passengers, intent only on their reading or catnapping.

But one Friday last summer, the airline figured out a way to get our collective attention. The pilot announced that he could not get the landing gear down and that we did not have enough fuel to continue circling the airport. The same stewardess we had completely disregarded earlier now commanded our rapt attention, and her words constituted the only message our ears wanted to hear. As we prepared to make a belly landing, we were more than interested in the locations of the exits. Recognizing fire engines, ambulances, and other emergency vehicles scurrying below us, we had a sudden interest in her knowledge of any position we could assume to reduce bodily damage upon impact. After our safe landing, we instinctively applauded our attendant and the unseen pilot she represented.

In the same way, teens-in-transition are more likely to regard a message that could rescue them and to give their allegiance to a Christ who answers crises. Teenagers are so life-oriented that when death takes someone close to them, they are deeply jarred and often become more receptive to the comforting love of an empathetic God.

I became a Christian after my grandmother's death in December. I woke up and found my mom sitting in her bedroom crying. When she told me that her mother had passed away in her sleep, I ran into my room screaming and crying out at God. "Why did she have to die? It's not fair!" After awhile, I quieted down and my mom talked to me about where my grandmother was and how I could join her someday.

—KARI, 15

I accepted Jesus at my mother's funeral.—EDWARD, 17

I think I already believed in God and heaven and hell, but I never really took it to heart until my cousin died from a blood clot in his brain that exploded.—ROB, 16

When I was thirteen years old, my father died. I knew I needed a different father. So I prayed with a friend and accepted Christ as my Savior. Now I have the best Father of all.—FRANK, 14

I was hired to work after school in a shoe store owned by a Christian couple. The district manager was also a Christian and would always take out his Bible and share verses with me. But I never understood what he was getting at until my best friend was killed in an auto accident. I realized that it could have been me in the car, and if it had been, I would have gone to hell. I wept and asked Jesus into my heart that night.—VALERIE, 17

DYING TO FIND CHRIST

Church-related teens are not immune to suicide. In fact, religious adolescents may be even more susceptible to suicidal thoughts than non-religious ones, claims Tom Burklow, director of Pastoral Counseling Services in Wayne, New Jersey. He reasons that

"Christian kids may feel like they want to be in heaven with Jesus or with a loved one who died. Or their sensitized consciences may lead them to feel so bad about themselves because of their sins that they begin to believe they deserve to die."[2]

Eighteen-year-old Bill was a basketball star at his high school and fairly active in his church youth group. One evening he and some of the guys on his team went out "pranking" in their neighborhood. While ripping open trash bags and emptying their leaves into the street, the boys were surprised by a patrolling squad car. Bill was gently escorted to the police station and briefly detained until his father's arrival. The humiliated father ordered his son to resign immediately from the school basketball team. The next day Bill went to a relative's garage, shut the door, climbed behind the wheel, rolled up the windows and turned on the engine. There he sat until the carbon monoxide ended his life.

The incident that triggers a teen's death wish is often fairly trivial. Karen, pretty, popular, the daughter of missionaries, and at fifteen not even old enough for a learner's permit, was prodded by a friend to take the family car. With parents away for the weekend, she wrecked the automobile. Miraculously uninjured, she got a lift home, scribbled a suicide note, and swallowed all the pills in the medicine chest. They merely put her to sleep. In the morning she wrote a second note which read, "There was just no other way out of this because you would be so disappointed in me. I love you, I love you." Then Karen jumped off the balcony of her tenth-floor apartment.

Even though "only" 5,000-plus suicides are reported yearly in the United States, Dr. Seymour Perlin, chairman of the National Youth Suicide Center in Washington D.C., reports that "as many as two million people between the ages of thirteen and nineteen will attempt suicide each year."[3] In a large-scale survey of California teens, psychologist Norman Farberow, co-director of the Los Angeles Suicide Prevention Center, found that each teenager in the thirteen-to-fifteen age group claimed that two out of five of his or her friends had been suicidal; in the sixteen-to-nineteen age group, the number jumped to three out of five.[4] One survey done among high school and college students asked the question, "Do you ever think suicide is an option?" Forty-nine percent responded, "Yes."[5]

If this research is accurate, then the ratio of teens who attempt suicide to those who commit it is almost 400 to 1. I have found that most teens who attempt suicide are particularly open to God's love in Christ when shared by a caring friend, parent, or youth pastor. Understanding this phenomenon prepared me for the many teens in my survey who reported becoming Christians after a suicide attempt.

I was a non-Christian, and my life was falling apart. So one night I tried to kill myself by overdosing on prescription drugs. When I woke up the next day, the youth pastor from our church was there. He told me how God wanted me alive, and I accepted Christ into my heart.

—LINDA, 16

My mother almost died from toxic shock syndrome in April. Then in September she had her second miscarriage. It was all too much for me. I was going through such total mental hell that I decided to kill myself. But my best friend heard my mental cry and made me go on a youth retreat with her church. It was there that I became a Christian and found a reason to go on living."—DARBY, 15

I was on the verge of suicide. I thought that no one cared about me at all. I had no place to go and no friends. I was not accepted into the crowd at school. I was a loner. And so I figured, why not . . . why not kill myself. It's not worth the trouble, and everyone will be a whole lot better off. The very evening that I was going to do it, I happened to see a movie called The Question *which was all about suicide and how much God loved us enough to send Jesus to die for our sins. I couldn't believe the coincidence. My whole outlook and attitude about life has changed since then.—LANCE, 17*

If almost every other teenager seriously contemplates suicide at some time between ages thirteen and nineteen, the chances that you will be in close contact with one of them, perhaps in your own home, run fairly high. "Friends and family members who spot suicidal signs should not be afraid of confronting the person," advises Mitch Anthony, founder of the National Suicide Help Center in Rochester, Minnesota. He continues, "Trust your intuition. People who are suicidal want to be rescued. They don't really want to die; they just don't know how to keep living with all that pain. Another person can help them deal with the pain."[6]

Most parents think that if you talk about suicide, you will increase the likelihood of it happening. The opposite is true. Denying, avoiding, or ignoring the problem increases the danger. Talking about the problem is a step toward solving it.

"One misconception people have," asserts Dr. Lawrence Kerns, a Chicago-area psychiatrist, "is that you can't see suicide coming. On the contrary, most suicidal teens manifest a variety of warning signals."[7]

Most families that I work with will say, "It was so impulsive, so sudden. We just had no way of knowing. There were no warning signs."

But then I ask, "Did he eat or sleep too much, or too little? Did he become more withdrawn? Was there a marked personality shift?"

Many parents reply, "I guess he was giving us some signals." It is both common and tragic that parents are often the last to perceive the depth of the problem. Parents should watch for the following signals:

- suicide threats or suicide plans
- severe depression, low self-esteem, hopelessness, unreasonable sense of pathological guilt, social withdrawal, listlessness, insomnia
- giving away prized possessions
- dramatic, sudden change in mood, in either direction
- acquisition of weapons, drugs, or firearms.

According to youth counselor Diane Eble, parents, pastors, and concerned friends should be alert to teenagers who are members of these high-risk categories:

- those who have gone through, or are going through, a family crisis. Approximately seventy-one percent of teens who attempt suicide are from broken homes. A recent study showed that many teens feel guilty and responsible for the breakup of their parents' marriage. Because they feel that things might work out if they were "out of the way," a suicide attempt can readily follow.
- those who have been abused physically, sexually, verbally, or through neglect. The number of students that I counsel who have been significantly abused in some manner has more than tripled in the past decade. The high correlation between teenagers who have been sexually abused and

those who attempt suicide is common knowledge among researchers.

- those who are facing the anniversary of a difficult loss (death, divorce, breakup of a romance)—especially when there has been sexual involvement.

- those who have previously attempted suicide. Four out of five teenagers who kill themselves this year will have made an attempt to do so before. It is common, however, for parents not to have any knowledge of these previous attempts. One girl reported, "I tried to end my life by taking a bunch of pills, but they just made me really sick. My parents and my friends at school thought I had the flu or something."

- those who feel pressure to excel. Such pressure may be external, applied by parents who have unrealistic expectations for their teens, or internal, created by adolescents who are perfectionists or hyper-critical of themselves. Particularly susceptible are sensitive, bright, often articulate church-related teenagers. Acutely aware of God's high standards, these teens often develop a distorted sense of their own sinfulness, and suicide can seem like a viable escape from their inability to measure up. Teens with this performance-orientation must be evangelized by focusing on the God who loves them in spite of their imperfections.[8]

God delights in taking "not many mighty, not many noble" (I Corinthians 1:26, NASB); instead He calls all of us who feel foolish and inadequate—simply because He loves us. A colleague of mine recently exclaimed, "Aren't you grateful that God created us as 'human beings' and not as 'human doings?' He loves us not because we 'do,' but because we 'are.' "

This message of unconditional love is good news for teens whose contemplation of suicide is triggered by their feelings of inadequacy and loneliness.

WHAT'S A PARENT TO DO?

This study reveals that God often uses crises to lead teenagers to a salvation experience with the Lord Jesus Christ. The concerned

Christian parent can play a significant role in this redemptive process.

1. Stop being a rescuer and allow your teen the chance to grow through suffering.

"Dear brothers, is your life full of difficulties and temptations? Then be happy, for when the way is rough, your patience has a chance to grow. So let it grow, and don't try to squirm out of your problems. . . . Then you will be ready for anything, strong in character, full and complete" (James 1:2-4, TLB).

I am always tempted to rescue my children from any experience of pain. But to protect them from difficult times is to perpetuate their spiritual immaturity and rob God of the opportunity to reach them during a crisis. "For remember," says Peter, "when your body suffers, sin loses its power, and you won't be spending the rest of your life chasing after evil desires, but will be anxious to do the will of God" (I Peter 4:1, 2, TLB).

Psychotherapist June Toellner claims that "most seriously rebellious adolescents were overprotected as children."[9] What does overprotection look like in Christian parents? It might be as simple as writing phony excuses for the teen who oversleeps and is often late for school. Sometimes Christian parents become habitual rescuers of their teens because, consciously or not, they feel guilty for having made their own regretful mistakes. The gnawing sense that they haven't been the parents they should have been contributes to the worst error parents can make. "I'll do all these things for my teen because I've been deficient in so many other ways," they resolve.

But if teens are protected from difficult situations, they may never understand God's offer of salvation. God said of the Hebrew children in Egyptian slavery, "I have indeed seen the misery of my people in Egypt. I have heard them crying out . . . and I am concerned about their suffering. So I have come down to rescue them . . ." (Exodus 3:7, 8). If parents insist on rescuing their children from the valleys that are common to all of us, they should not be surprised when those teens express no interest in God as rescuer. It would seem they have no need of Him.

2. Use the time of crisis as an opportunity to draw closer to your teen.

"A friend loves at all times, and a brother is born for adversity" (Proverbs 17:17).

I hardly knew my neighbor across the street until the creek behind his house flooded one chilly night in March. The next morning he was at my door with a pathetic look on his face and an understated, "I think I need your help."

We spent the rest of the day together battling nature gone berserk, as the raging torrent jumped its boundaries and encroached upon his home. Floating his refrigerator out the patio door and down the block to dry ground, salvaging whatever articles that remained above the water level, wading chest deep in the freezing, murky depths that claimed the entire lower level of his house, we experienced a unique camaraderie that can only be born in a crisis. I am convinced that I would have never really known my taciturn neighbor, and more importantly, never have had the opportunity to lead him to a salvation experience with Jesus Christ, if that flood crisis had not brought us together.

God has done so much good by starting with something difficult that, as a Christian parent, I almost look forward to times of crisis because I know that opportunities for deep communication and spiritual contact with my teens usually accompany them. In the daily routine of being a Christian family, the chance seldom arises to have profound conversations that will impact your teen morally and spiritually.

No matter how well intended, moral preaching can hardly compete with boyfriends, girlfriends, athletic events, school activities, and homework for a teen's attention. Day-to-day contact with your teenager must be characterized more by right living than by right talking.

But when a teen is arrested for shoplifting at the local mall, when his heart is broken by a shattered romantic relationship, when she discovers why her period is late this month, when he awakens with a headache from getting drunk with some school friends the night before, or when her depression has led her to thoughts of suicide, both you and God have an excellent opportunity to do significant spiritual business with your teen.

The ground that is broken up is most receptive to the seed.

3. Persevere in your marriage relationship.

"If a Christian woman has a husband who isn't a Christian, and he wants her to stay with him, she must not leave him . . .

Otherwise, if the family separates, the children might never come to know the Lord" (I Corinthians 7:13, 14a, TLB).

That a large majority of youth who try to take their own lives come from broken homes would seem enough of a reason for you to persevere in your marriage. But the apostle Paul encourages us to stay with our mates because "a united family may, in God's plan, result in the children's salvation" (I Corinthians 7:14b, TLB).

Teenagers from Christian homes with both spouses have a better chance of making a decision to follow Jesus Christ than those from broken homes. Before either mate chooses self over family, he or she would do well to consider Elwood McQuaid's "The Divorce."

> *"It's just not there anymore," he told her. "Oh, I loved you once, but all we do is fight. The kids will be okay, better off really. They can come on weekends and stay two months in the summer. Yes, I'll support you, count on that. Keep the house, all I want's the car. No, there's no one else—what kind of person do you think I am?" He knew he was lying, and she thought so.*
>
> *The door was closed on many things that day. For he did not leave just a wife, you see. It wasn't okay with the kids. And they weren't better off. They did not endorse his leaving them— neither did his God. Snatches of fatherhood in company with a stranger could not salve his guilt or serve to satisfy their need.*
>
> *When it's all over and done with, both of them gone from the earthly scene, where will the kids take theirs to remember? There is no family place with granite markers side by side. There is no family. Lust saw to that years before. So her remains rest here, while his are far away, placed beside another—or maybe just alone.*[10]

It is too easy to terminate a marriage in contemporary society. Legal grounds for divorce are abundant and range from impotence to incompatibility to "refusal by mate to move to a new residence"! Our Lord Jesus specified only adultery as justification for divorce, and even then did not command it, but left room for forgiveness and restoration. The spiritual receptivity of your teenagers is more than worth the effort.

Still, close to one out of every two readers of this book has experienced divorce. Dann Spader addresses this crisis in the home by challenging those of us with healthy home lives to become "substitute parents" for needy teens. He says, "Today over fifty percent of teens are from broken homes. As we seek to model and imitate God's love to us, it will cause us to reach out and in love seek to 'adopt' those teens who need to experience that love. Through that reflecting of God's character, it would be our desire to see these young people become a part of God's family."[11]

4. Without minimizing the consequences, minister hope to your teen.

"Yea, though I walk through the valley of the shadow of death. . . Thou art with me" (Psalm 23:4, KJV).

Just as they can be too flippant about the consequences of their bad choices, so teenagers often err on the opposite extreme by becoming harmfully morose when hope is unduly postponed. I saw this problem with one of my own children.

About a year after I had written *Keeping Your Teen in Touch with God*, my wife and I entered a period of being stretched and tested by our teens. One of them, after getting caught in a lie and breaking a major house rule, slipped a greeting card under my bedroom door. It had been a few days since the infraction, and I had noticed that a spirit of despondency had settled over this teen and our house in general. On the front of the card was a picture of a guilty-looking cat standing beside the mangled arm of a couch he had just used as a pin cushion for his claws. Inside the card were these impassioned words:

> *Dear Dad,*
> *I know you're going to have a hard time believing anything I say or even caring about what I say, but I'm really sorry. I feel like scum. I realize how my selfishness has caused you and Mom a lot of pain. I know it will be a long time before I can ever earn your trust back. I'm not trying to justify anything, but I think that all the feelings I've ever had about how hard it is to be the child of a minister hit me at once. And all of a sudden I just wanted to stop being Bob Laurent's "teen in touch with God." I wish that I didn't love my family so much so that I could just run away or something. I've even caught myself thinking that it would have been better if I'd gotten into a fatal car wreck that night. I guess it's all a lot deeper than just saying that I'm stupid, irresponsible, and untrustworthy. I don't even know if you can accept my apology, but I'm sorry, and I really do love you.*

There is a time for silence, when you allow your teenagers the opportunity to hear God's voice speaking to them in their pain, but there is never a time for withdrawal. There is a time for observation and prayer, but there is also a time for rescue and hope. It seemed to me that this was just such a time for our family.

Even in the midst of Jerusalem's destruction, when he was crying, "My soul is downcast within me!," Jeremiah remembered God's love for him and had hope. "Because of the Lord's great love we are not consumed, for his compassions never fail. Great is your faithfulness." (Lamentations 3:22, 23).

During times of crisis, we need to show our teenagers a love that never fails. Their salvation may depend upon it.

CHAPTER
10

The Passing of the Age of Innocence

The Impact of the Media on a Teenager's Faith

Now that we are learning to recycle our trash, how about recycling our forms of entertainment?
—RICHARD NEVILLE

O F THE TEENS I SURVEYED, almost ten percent of those who made decisions for Christ during adolescence (103 out of 1,068) were directly influenced to do so by Christian music, movies, or television. After hearing testimonies like the following, Christian recording artists should be encouraged to continue writing music that focuses on the lordship of Christ.

I became a Christian at a Myron LeFevre/Broken Heart concert. When they were singing "We Are His Hands," I gave my heart to Jesus Christ.—TOM, 15

My boss's son is a Christian, and he bought a Petra tape for me and my brother. Well, my brother liked it a lot, but I told him to quit playing that tape around me. All I cared about was Dungeons and Dragons, Def Lepard, and AC/DC. But over the summer I became extremely depressed, and I told my parents that there was nothing in life to look forward to. One night in August, when I was at the end of my rope, the words on Petra's tape kept coming back to me, and I totally turned my life over to God.—LARRY, 16

It was at a Whiteheart concert that I finally realized I didn't really know the Lord. Because of their music, I saw that going through all the motions of Christianity didn't make any real difference; accepting Christ did.—PAM, 15

Contemporary Christian music can have a powerful evangelistic impact on teenagers. In fact, when I asked the 1,200 church-related teens in this study to name the best way to reach their non-Christian friends, over half of them cited, "Christian music/concerts." One boy wrote, "Good ol' Christian rock 'n roll is the best way to reach teenagers for Jesus Christ. They can relate to it because that kind of music is a part of their world, and they'll listen to it if it's done well. For the same reason that God became a man to relate to us, I think the Church should put its message in the form of Christian rock to relate to non-Christian teens."

He has a good point, doesn't he? In fact, his logic resembles Paul's in I Corinthians 9:22, "Whatever a person is like, I try to find common ground with him so that he will let me tell him about Christ and let Christ save him"(TLB).

Such is the great opportunity that the Christian media have among America's teenagers. Truth that a parent or pastor has a difficult time imparting to a teen, a movie with redemptive values often successfully communicates. Teenagers love to go to the movies. For some of them, it can mean a life-changing contact with Jesus Christ.

I decided I wanted to be a Christian after I went to youth group and saw a movie called Without Reservation. *I was really moved by it because it talked about heaven and hell and how you never know when you'll die. I knew that if I died, I wanted to go to heaven.*—ALAN, 16

I saw the movie Jesus of Nazareth *on TV and it made me realize that I didn't have the Messiah as my Lord. By myself, in my bedroom, I gave my whole self to Jesus. I've been growing ever since.*—PHILIP, 17

I had gone to church since I was a baby, but I never understood the meaning of it. Then one Sunday night, we watched A Thief in the Night, *and it inspired me to give my life to Christ.*—SONJA, 16

THE LOSS OF INNOCENCE

I often advise parents not to argue with their teens over non-essentials so that they will have both a stable friendship with the youth and enough emotional reserve for those issues that are worth the price of confrontation. The negative influence of the media is just such an issue. Although God has used music, movies, and television to evangelize teenagers, the negative influence of these media forms on a teen's faith is by far outstripping their positive impact.

We don't have many rules at our house, but most of them stand guard against the encroachment of the secular media on the minds of our children. The seduction of the adolescent mind is a battlefield worthy of any Christian parent's involvement.

During a recent conversation with sixteen-year-old Michelle, a member of the National Honor Society and a cheerleader at her high school, I was reminded of the high stakes for which we parents are playing.

"You baby boomers are an interesting breed," she said, telling me that she had just read an essay about how people of my generation still react so strongly to the day that John F. Kennedy was assassinated. "Your generation lost its innocence on November 22, 1963." After a short pause, she reflected, "But my generation has no innocence to lose. And if what my generation has now is innocence, it frightens me to think of what our version of November 22nd will be."

Then out of nowhere she said, "I wish I'd been born in 1950. Then when I turned seventeen, it would be 1967 instead of 1991."

"Why in the world would you wish that?" I asked.

"I may be wrong," she said, "but my impression of that time is that the only things kids worried about was who they were going to go out with, or if their homework was done, or what the new songs were. But today I know kids working after school and at nights so that they can give money to their moms, because their dads have left home. And kids worrying about getting busted for going into a bar underage, and seventh-grade girls on the pill so they won't get pregnant, and fourth-grade kids being pressured to do drugs."

Her dark eyes flashed as she looked up at me and said, "Just think back to when you were in grade school. Can you imagine a kid coming to school stoned or drunk?"

"I don't believe things were as good as you think they were when I was your age," I replied. "But I agree with you that they've gotten a lot worse through the years. This is a tough time to be a teenager."

Not really expecting her to have the answer, I asked her a question anyway. "Why do you think it's so hard to be a teen today, Michelle?"

This bright young lady from a non-Christian home answered, "Do you really want to know? I think it's because we've become incredibly jaded so early. I mean, we've seen everything by the time we're fifteen or sixteen. We can turn on cable TV and see people in bed together anytime we want. Nothing shocks us anymore. We listen to music for hours everyday that tells us to surrender to our glands and live for ourselves. We've come too far too fast."

I think Michelle is right. Today's generation of teenagers has no innocence to lose. The media already seduced them in their pre-teen years. And Christian parents who are concerned about the spiritual condition of their teens need to understand the dangerous media influences these youth face daily. Following is a briefing on the negative impact that music, movies, and television have on our children, along with some helpful advice for parents.

ROCK 'N' ROLL: AN INDUSTRY GONE MAD

Paul King, M.D., author of *Sex, Drugs, and Rock 'n' Roll*, recently testified before a U.S. Senate subcommittee that "heavy metal is America's newest religion."[1] Housewife and mother Phyllis Roberson has taken the satanic rock group Judas Priest to court over their album, *Stay In Class*. She claims that the album incites teenagers to take their own lives, and she should know. Immediately after listening to it, her son, Raymond, and his best friend, James Vance, ended their lives by putting a sawed-off shotgun to their heads.

Wilson Bryan Key, an expert on subliminal messages, testified that the album in question consisted of four songs about satanism, two promoting suicide, and one that appealed to teens to throw off all parental authority. He stated that the subliminal phrase, "Do it!" was hidden throughout the lyrics and constituted an encouragement to listeners to commit suicide.

Mrs. Roberson reported that after intense involvement with

heavy metal, her son was growing deeply depressed. She confided that during his struggle, "I used to sit with him at night and sing church hymns to him just to get the satanic music out of his head so that he could sleep. But it was too late. One day he went to the churchyard, sat on a merry-go-round, and pulled the trigger."[2]

"Something has snapped in the judgment of corporate America," claims Bob DeMoss, youth culture specialist for Focus on the Family. "They reason that the only way to make a buck in a morally numb society is to outshock the competition—regardless of the sociological consequences."[3]

To reach teenagers with their products, large corporations are sponsoring outrageous musical groups like 2 Live Crew, Madonna, and George Michael. They are focusing over seventy percent of their advertising budgets on the teenage market, reasoning that youth will identify with today's pop idols enough to buy whatever they are selling.[4]

Still, the sixty-plus billion dollars that teenagers spent in 1990 is not my major concern as a Christian parent. It is the inescapable reality that American teens by the millions are falling in line behind role models who present values in direct opposition to those of the homes in which they were raised.

Madonna is the self-proclaimed high priestess of teenage sex. She has always attempted to integrate her confused religious beliefs with her steamy sensuality. Her public statements that "Nuns are sexy" and "Crucifixes are sexy, because there's a naked man on them" shocked her early followers.[5] But no one is shocked these days.

In her song, "Hanky Panky," she endorses both physical abuse and sexual bondage. Sample lines: "Tie my hands behind my back and o-o-h, I'm in ecstasy," and "I'll settle for the back of your hand, somewhere on my behind." Bob DeMoss reports that, "On her tour, Madonna simulated sex acts on stage. Male dancers wore bras and simulated the fondling of their breasts. Meanwhile, executives at Warner Brothers counted their profits."[6]

Madonna's male counterpart in the sexploitation of American teenagers is George Michael. Particularly dangerous because he couches his songs about sex in religious terms, the handsome Michael entitled his latest album *Faith*. But to Michael, "faith" means believing that there is always another lover just around the corner. The magazine *Youthworker* disclosed the dangers of Michael's lyrics.

"In [the song] 'Father Figure,' it is sex that makes him a preacher/teacher, and what he holds sacred is the warm and naked body of his young disciple. In 'I Want Your Sex,' he finds revelation because his passion tells him what's true ('Don't need no Bible, just look in my eyes/I won't tell you lies'). In another song, he promises to take his lover to 'The Edge of Heaven.' But the song adds a sadomasochistic twist to the Gospel. There is probably no more vital prophet for the sex-as-religion cult in music today."[7]

Many parents would like to believe that their teens are not picking up on the psycho-sexual implications of these songs. However, research on the sexual patterns of church-related teenagers proscribes such optimism. Josh McDowell reveals that forty-three percent of conservative Christian teenagers have experienced sexual intercourse before high school graduation.[8]

This dismaying statistic begs at least the following crucial question: If religiously oriented teens have been taught for the first decade of their lives that sexual intercourse is a gift from God, only to be practiced within the confines of a Christian marriage, what pressure could be strong enough to cause almost half of them to fly in the face of their upbringing? What force outside the home could be potent enough to convince them to disregard the inherent dangers and risk certain conflict with their own parents and the church? Dave Hart, in "Pop Music's Unholy Trinity," claims that the answer is obvious. "So where do they learn that sex is such a valuable and viable activity? Almost every applicable study shows they are learning these ideas from the media."[9]

WHAT'S A PARENT TO DO?

1. Familiarize yourself with the secular rock scene.

"And do this, understanding the present time. The hour has come for you to wake up from your slumber" (Romans 13:11a).

One of my first experiences with MTV (music television) came at a parsonage in central California, where I was spending the week with a pastor and his family while conducting evening services at their church. I sensed that something was wrong after he greeted me upon my arrival at his home and introduced me to his wife.

"We, uh, have a sixteen-year-old son," he offered, with a note of apology in his voice. "But you probably won't see much of him this week."

"Oh, why not?" I asked. "Did I drive him away already?"

"No, he's here at the house," he replied. "He just spends a lot of time in his room."

Little did I know what an understatement this hard-working pastor and troubled parent had just made. During a full week of meetings, none of which the young man attended, I saw his son a total of three times—once for about five uncomfortable minutes at the dinner table and twice after I knocked on his bedroom door and asked if I could talk with him.

When this kid was not at school, he locked the world out of his bedroom and watched MTV on a twenty-five inch screen for hours a day. I had never met a more reclusive, anti social teen in my life.

When he unlocked the door and grudgingly allowed me to enter his inner sanctum, I walked in on the middle of a Guns 'n Roses rock video and soon understood something about this young man's behavior. I had interrupted him as he was watching a girl being raped and murdered to the driving background lyrics, "I used to love her, but I had to kill her."

At first, I was so shaken I could not react. This was not "American Bandstand." I was simultaneously angry, frightened, and over-whelmed as I realized how pathetically out of touch I was with what teenagers were listening to. That day I determined to learn enough about the rock scene to be able to minister to kids who were caught up in it.

The typical adolescent absorbs between three and five hours of rock music every day. How long can even a Christian teen hold out under such a steady bombardment of sex, drugs, satanic ritual, and suicide? The chances are good that I am not the only parent who knew little about the mind-bending genre of heavy metal rock. To understand its lethal effect on a teenager's faith is a start for the concerned parent. It is a phenomenon worth fighting.

2. Let your teens have their own Christian music.

"Avoid foolish controversies . . . because these are unprofitable and useless" (Titus 3:9).

Research has shown the "generation gap" largely to be a myth. Laurence Steinberg writes in *Adolescence*, "When we look at intergenerational differences in values and attitudes, we find little evidence in support of a generation gap—or at least, of a schism as large as many people have been led to believe exists. . . . To date, no studies demonstrate that family problems are any more likely to occur during adolescence than at other times in the life span."[10]

The good news is that teens and their parents have similar beliefs about life and the personal characteristics and attitudes they feel are important. When it comes to basic values and attitudes, the generations are closer than most parents would suppose. The bad news is that many parents risk their relationships with teenagers by bickering over matters of personal taste. Preference in style of music is not worth that risk.

In the God-ordained process of becoming self-actualized, adolescents need to have autonomy in the areas of preference and taste. It is both psychologically and spiritually healthy for teens to have their own forms of expression; choosing their own style of music is wholesome. If the message of the music is Christian, then the wise parent should be thankful to God that his teen is being influenced by Michael W. Smith, Amy Grant, and Stephen Curtis Chapman instead of Motley Crue, Def Lepard, and 2 Live Crew.

3. Enlist your teens in a mission to clean up the spiritual atmosphere of your home.

"Come now, let us reason together . . ." (Isaiah 1:18).

Years ago, when our children were very young, Joyce and I read Matthew 18:10 ("See that you do not look down on one of these little ones. For I tell you that their angels in heaven always see the face of my Father in heaven") and took it seriously. We neither pray to angels nor worship them (Colossians 2:18), but we do keep an understanding of their existence alive in our family.

We reasoned that if angels lived in our home, and it was one of their major responsibilities to watch over our children, then we should be grateful enough to do everything possible to make them feel welcome. We began to build in our family a sense of awareness to the marvelous angelic beings God sends to our home as "ministering spirits sent to serve those who will inherit salvation" (Hebrews 1:14).

Buying all the praise music tapes we could find, we learned where the Christian station was on our radio dial and resolved to play nothing that would offend our heavenly companions. So from the early days, we have enlisted our children to help us in maintaining the spiritual atmosphere of our home. This custom has the double benefit of keeping a check on the music we play and giving each child a sense of mission and ownership, and has given us more leverage than the average parent, who is often reduced to harmful shouting matches over musical content.

4. Consecrate the musical equipment in your home to God.

". . . A man [shall dedicate] his house as something holy to the Lord" (Leviticus 27:14).

One of our most important traditions occurs whenever a stereo or compact disc player is purchased for any member of the family. Gathering in a little "holy huddle," we inaugurate its addition to our home with a brief time of prayer. Just as all instruments in Solomon's temple were sanctified ("set apart") for ministry before the Lord, so we dedicate the musical machinery that sets the spiritual tone for our household.

"Lord, we love You and we respect one another," we pray. "Give us wisdom not to use this boom box to play anything that would offend the Holy Spirit or welcome the forces of darkness into our home."

5. Offer "amnesty" to the teen involved in heavy metal.

"Bear with each other and forgive whatever grievances you may have against one another" (Colossians 3:13a, KJV).

Many Christian families do not have the opportunity of establishing musical standards in the home when their children are pre-teens. Can anything be done for the home whose teenagers are already heavily involved in secular rock? The answer is "yes." God expects us to work with the amount of light that we've been given.

If you approach your teenagers with respect and genuine love, the chances are good that they will give you a fair hearing. It is important that you explain with clarity and kindness the reasons behind your decisions, and ask them to help you in the task of making your home a Christian one. Bob DeMoss suggests that at this point, you could offer your teens an "amnesty policy" in which you buy back from them (at a depreciated rate) all the cassettes, videotapes, posters, etc. which don't measure up to the family standards. Also, since teens are so often short of money, and with CDs costing between twelve and twenty dollars, it might be worth it to parents to pay for half of a Christian tape if the teen pays the other half.

DeMoss offers another provocative thought you should consider before meeting with your teen: "Some parents lecture their children about the 'evils of rock,' but then watch their own form of evil. Teens rightly argue, what is the difference between Bon Jovi singing 'Living in Sin' and my parents watching J. R. Ewing committing adultery on 'Dallas'?"[11]

In the words of Dr. James C. Dobson, "Values are caught, not taught."

6. Encourage your teens to form their own Christian musical group.

"Do not be overcome by evil, but overcome evil with good" (Romans 12:21).

One of the greatest ways to fight the influence of secular rock on our teens is to encourage them to start their own Christian bands. Such an experience not only evangelizes other teenagers with great effect, but allows the Holy Spirit to have a deep, faith-strengthening impact on the members of the musical group as they are used by God to minister to others.

MOVIES AND TELEVISION: HORROR, PORN, AND PAIN

More grade-school children recognize mass murderer Freddy Krueger of the gruesome *Nightmare on Elm Street* film series than they do Abraham Lincoln.[12] "Slasher films" constitute the most popular genre of movies among teenagers today, including church-related teens.

In one episode of the Nightmare series, a young woman is chased down by a group of teenage boys. She is thrown into a shack with dead bodies of other women who had been caught and are hanging on meat hooks. She escapes and flags down a truck. She thinks the guys in the truck are her rescuers; instead, they rape her and throw her out on the road. Then another truck runs her over. At the end of the movie Freddy, with his long claws, comes on to cackle and enjoy this sadism.

"And this," claims Dr. Thomas Radecki, founder of the National Coalition on Television Violence, "is aimed at a teen and pre-teen audience!"[13] According to Radecki, television is no better.

- A research study published in the *American Journal of Epidemiology* concluded that "Television is a factor in approximately 10,000 homicides each year in the United States."[14]

- Excessive TV viewing not only causes obesity and violent behavior in children, it encourages them to engage in irresponsible sexual conduct and promotes abuse of alcohol, according to the American Academy of Pediatrics.[15]

- Children's programs contain nearly five times more violent acts than do prime-time shows, researchers found in the continuing study, "Violence Profile 1967-1990: Enduring Patterns." The "Profile" disclosed that during children's hours, ninety percent of the programs are violent.

In San Leandro, California, a twelve-year-old boy raped his five-year-old sister after watching a sex scene on television on Sunday. "He said he got the idea while watching TV the day before at his aunt's house," police Lt. Thomas Hull told the Associated Press.

"Television did not invent violence," one report stated. "It just put it on the assembly line and into every home."[16] Research speaks with one voice. Teenagers who are raised on heavy doses of TV violence will cultivate a sense of relative danger, mistrust, dependence, alienation, and gloom. The more hours of TV they watch, the more prevalent these feelings will be.

Because we are human, it is our nature to become parents who compromise. Media offerings that might have deeply offended us a few years ago, we tolerate today and will probably endorse tomorrow. We have become morally desensitized by our apathy and inertia.

Franky Schaeffer sounds a clarion call to all Christian parents: "Christians have become far too well behaved. Our silence and non-involvement must stop. We must once again commit ourselves to a robust view of truth. Religious people must once again become involved in every area of life: politics, law, medicine, family life, education, science, the media, and the arts. . . . Where are the Christian men and women to stand up and fight without compromise?"

Schaeffer concludes, "There are times in which anyone with a shred of moral principle should be profoundly angry. We live in such times."[17]

WHAT'S A PARENT TO DO?

Regarding the debased state of today's secular media, we simply must love our teens enough to get angry. "So [Jesus] made a whip out of cords, and drove all from the temple . . . His disciples remembered that it is written: 'Zeal for your house will consume me' " (John 2:15, 17).

In Paddy Chayefsky's story of a network news anchorman who suffers an emotional breakdown during the evening news program, the tragic figure issues a crazed but well-received challenge to his viewers. He looks into the camera and pleads, "I don't know what to do about all of the problems in this world. All I know is first you've got to get mad. Right now. I want you to go to the window, open it, and stick your head out and yell. I want you to yell: 'I'm mad as h— and I'm not going to take this anymore!'"[18]

God tells us to "hate evil, and love the good" (Amos 5:15, TLB). David Seamands wrote, "The man who cannot get angry about evil worries me, because he is the same man who really doesn't have a lot of enthusiasm for good and for righteousness. If you cannot hate evil, if you cannot become angry about certain situations in the world today, then it is very questionable that you really love righteousness and holiness."[19]

There is a great battle being fought over the airwaves for the souls of our teenagers, and most of the secular media are not on the side of Christian parents. God is waiting for those who love teenagers to get angry enough to act on their beliefs. Perhaps it is time to go to the window, open it, and stick your head out, and yell: "I'm mad as HEAVEN, and I'm not going to take this anymore!"

Some very practical things that parents can do are:

1. Videotape an offensive program and send it to the FCC (Federal Communications Commission, Complaints and Investigative Branch, Enforcement Division, 2025 M St. N.W., Washington, DC, 20554).

It would also be productive to send copies of any program you believe violates the FCC decency standard to the owners of the stations as well and to the advertisers. The American Family Association keeps a record of the advertisers. (The AFA can be reached at P.O. Box 2440, Tupelo, MS 38803.)

2. Request to be put on the mailing list of "Movieguide," a biweekly biblical guide to movies and entertainment. (Good News Communications, Inc., P.O. Box 9952, Atlanta, Georgia 30319)

3. Obtain a membership to "Parent Guidance," a newsletter advising parents how to oppose the destructive elements in youth culture. (Write Focus on the Family, P.O. Box 500, Pomona, CA 91769)

4. Either purge your home of a television set or learn to treat it like any other household appliance. Richard Fredericks reports that over thirty percent of our homes today are classified as "constant television families," meaning that the TV is never turned off during the day, even when no one is viewing it.[20]

It is rare when I visit a Christian home where the television is not the focal point of the household, reigning over whatever room the family spends most of its time in.

5. Pray for discernment for you and your teen. Bob DeMoss suggests that we teach our children a prayer that his parents taught him: "Help me to love what You love, Lord, and hate what You hate." He is convinced that this prayer prepared him to face a hostile youth culture and helped him to combat the negative influence of the media.

This chapter has revealed that positive media influence can have a powerful evangelistic impact on today's teens. Scores of the teenagers I interviewed cited Christian music, movies, or television as the agent that led them to Christ. But as with any phenomenon that can be wonderfully used by God, these agents can also be terribly twisted to serve the cause of evil. Via the media, our children will be exposed both to good and evil on almost a daily basis for the rest of their lives. My own prayer for my teens resembles Jesus' words in John 17:15: "My prayer is not that you take [our teenagers] out of the world but that you protect them from the evil one."

CHAPTER
11

From Doubt to Decision
Evangelizing by Answering a Teenager's Questions

If we don't honestly face the "why" questions in our churches, we will lose our young people.—JAY KESLER

A faith which today has to lean on authoritarianism and abstractions will collapse tomorrow under the pressure of cultural change.—DR. PIERRE BABIN

Every teenager must have the opportunity to experience Christianity as a rational, thinking faith that can stand up to the kind of honest questioning that typifies the adolescent mind. Teens' cognitive abilities have reached the stage of formal operations; they are fully capable of considering a myriad of possible ways to solve problems and are ready to reason on the basis of propositional logic.[1] It is only natural that they look at the claims of the Christian faith from several different perspectives and consider a variety of factors before making a decision.

Adolescent psychologist Richard Havighurst claims that one of the most crucial developmental tasks of adolescence is acquiring one's own set of values and a personal belief system to guide behavior.[2] There is no finer moment for Christian parents than when their son or daughter announces, "Mom and Dad, I'm no longer a Christian because it's what you believe. I'm a Christian because I believe in it."

"The kids on my danger list are those who have been told what to think but never taught how to think," says Christian educator David Baldwin. "Many of these kids drop out of church activities because they are saturated with a faith that has been forced on them, but is not their own. They reach a point where they simply refuse to perform."[3]

By suppressing their doubts, downplaying their questions, and encouraging blind belief, the church is unintentionally losing the chance for real Christianity to become an experiential part of the world view of teenagers. Sandy Larsen, in the article "Listening to Our Children That They Might Believe," contends, "Young people who cannot air contrary assumptions may never see Scripture stand up to opposition. When will they find out how well the Bible handles questions? Is biblical truth so unconvincing that we must guard it from encountering any other view?"[4]

Teenagers need a forum where their doubts can be discussed—a tough-minded Christianity that can deal with their real problems. When we parents dismiss their doubts, our teens learn that neither the home nor the church is a place where they can speak the truth, but where they must say what is expected. Meanwhile, they continue to cultivate their own opinions. Who is God? Just who is Jesus Christ? Does my life have any meaning?

Most teens inhabit their own suprachurch existence—the real world for which church is a weekly interruption to be tolerated. Larsen adds, "And if [a teen] has been raised carefully in the church, he is very good at looking like he really believes it all."[5]

Many Christian parents feel that questioning is a negative behavior, but I disagree. Questioning and doubting are integral parts of God's natural process for a teen and can be very positive experiences. I have often wondered why we are so threatened by their questions. Are we fearful and abrasive because we are fighting our own unbelief and shouting down our own denial? Are we fearful that God has no verity, or is too weak to defend Himself?

An important means of developing personal convictions about Christianity is by questioning. "In fact," claims Larry Richards, "if a young person doesn't question, he's likely to have more problems later on."[6]

The Lord Jesus is not intimidated by our teens' need to be true to their stage of cognitive development. On the contrary, the sixth leading reason teenagers gave for following Jesus Christ was that, in the Christian faith, they found answers to their questions and doubts.

I accepted Jesus Christ as my Lord and Savior when I was thirteen. I was being pressured a lot by my parents, but that was just driving me away. However, with the help of a very godly woman in my youth group,

I really started to understand what Christianity was all about. She took the time to disciple me and that's when a lot of my questions were answered.—MANDY, 13

One of the more profound responses came from a fifteen-year-old daughter of a preacher.

I grew up hearing all the stories, so it only came natural to believe and accept them. His love was shown to me through my parents and the church. But when I became a teenager, I realized that it's only when you're on your own that your faith becomes more than an inheritance. I was struggling with God for various reasons, and I knew that the little faith I had wasn't mine. I had to go back to the beginning and find out if there really is a God. But He never let go of me, so I eventually found Him again. But that time was different, because I did it on my own. I wasn't being coached from the sidelines. It's only through doubting that God becomes ours.—CONNIE, 15

Several teens expressed their appreciation for Christians who were there to listen and answer their questions.

I kept asking questions about Christianity and finally saw that God was, in fact, real and that Jesus Christ was His Son. It took several conversations with some knowledgeable Christians for me to realize that you don't have to check your brain at the door when you accept Christ.

—MATT, 18

Starting in high school, I went through a long period of questioning my faith. I convinced myself that Christianity was for non-thinkers or old people facing death. Then I got interested in a girl who was a strong Christian. It seemed like she had an answer for every one of my questions about God and the Bible. I realized that Christianity was the truth.—DAVID, 16

I probably never would have become a Christian if my dad hadn't been able to answer my questions about Jesus, heaven, and hell.—TODD, 17

It seems obvious that teenagers need parents who will give them latitude to express their doubts and act as patient listeners to their questions. Those who are concerned about evangelizing their teens will heed the following advice.

WHAT'S A PARENT TO DO?

1. Never argue with your teen about their beliefs.

"Don't have anything to do with foolish and stupid arguments, because you know they produce quarrels" (II Timothy 2:23).

Because you are not the Holy Spirit, you can relinquish the burden you might feel for convincing your teenagers of their need to believe as you do about Christianity. "But when he, the Spirit of truth, comes, he will guide you into all truth" (John 16:13a).

Adolescents with normal willpower will naturally be inclined to reject a belief system that is forced upon them. They are inherently spoiling for a fight with anyone who attempts to make faith decisions for them that they know they must make for themselves. Verbal confrontations over personal beliefs will serve only further to alienate a teen who is considering Christianity as one of many options.

On the other hand, more than one Christian parent has disarmed and evangelized a belligerent teenager with patience and a quiet confidence that God, in His own good time and way, is working within that teen. The apostle Paul advised, ". . . the Lord's servant must not quarrel; instead he must be kind to everyone. . . . Those who oppose him he must gently instruct, in the hope that God will grant them repentance leading them to a knowledge of the truth" (II Timothy 2:24, 25).

2. Help your teen learn how to think.

"Then we will no longer be infants, tossed back and forth by the waves, and blown here and there by every wind of teaching. . . . Instead speaking the truth in love, we will in all things grow up into him" (Ephesians 4:14, 15a).

The last thing I want for my teens is for them to passively encode the messages they are being bombarded with daily by the media and secular society in general. Harry Blamires, in *The Christian Mind*, challenges parents to enable their teens to "think Christianly" about the world around them. By this he means that we should encourage our children to aggressively evaluate today's culture rather than hide them from it.

If we have taught them how to discern what is good from what is evil, then we can prayerfully launch them into a world that desperately needs the input their Christian minds can bring to it. But their entrance into a society where Christian truth must be addressed will most likely never occur until we have first given their own questions a fair hearing. How can we expect them to be able to think for themselves after they leave home if we have not taught them to think during their youth?

Jacques Ellul understands what is at stake here: "[Parents] must educate for risk and change. We must not shelter the young from the world's dangers, but arm them so that they will be able to overcome them. We are talking about arming them not with a legalistic breastplate, but with the strength of freedom. We are teaching them not to fight in their own strength, but to ask for the Holy Spirit and to rely on Him. Parents must be willing to allow their children to be placed in danger, knowing that there is no possible education in Christ without the presence of real dangers in the world, for without danger, Christian education is only a worthless pretty picture which will not help at all when children first meet up with concrete life."[7]

3. Prepare yourself to deal with their questions.

"Always be prepared to give an answer to everyone who asks you to give the reason for the hope that you have. But do this with gentleness and respect" (I Peter 3:15b).

After years of listening to teens, I have recognized five recurring questions they have. Following are typical situations which generate each question, and possible answers to equip parents for that time when their advice is sought.

Question #1. It seems that every time I want to have some fun, Christianity is there to spoil it. I'm getting tired of being told what I can't do. Why does Christianity have to be so negative?

I usually begin my answer to this question by suggesting to teens that they are probably not having problems with the person of Jesus Christ but with a form of religion that does not always represent Christianity. The Bible is filled with passages which support their conviction that faith should not be characterized by negativism and legalistic interpretations.

"... In [Jesus Christ] it has always been 'Yes.' For no matter how many promises God has made, they are 'Yes' in Christ." (II Corinthians 1:19b, 20)

"I have come that they may have life, and have it to the full." (John 10:10b)

"If the Son sets you free, you will be free indeed." (John 8:36)

"The letter [of the law] kills, but the Spirit gives life." (II Corinthians 3:6b)

Youth need to be introduced to a God who says *yes* to their passion for life. Jesus was labeled a "glutton and a drunkard" (Matthew 11:19) by his contemporaries because of his zest for life. He certainly never meant for teens to conclude that Christianity is a religion of rules and regulations.

When teenagers ask, "Who is Jesus?" and we answer by saying, "Don't do this! Don't touch that! Don't associate with them! Don't look at that! And for heaven's sake, don't even think that!"—how can a teen respond other than, "Don't bother me with your religion"?

However, freedom in Christ is not to be confused with license to break rules and live for oneself. The abundant life has always demanded a prerequisite for freedom, and that is obedience. "If you hold to my teaching, you are really my disciples. Then you will know the truth, and the truth will set you free" (John 8:31, 32).

Question #2. I have a teacher at school who claims that the Bible is a book full of errors and myths. How do I know the Bible is God's Word?

Whenever anyone informs me that, in his opinion, the Bible could not be the inspired Word of God because it is riddled with errors, I politely ask him to tell me which errors are causing him the most trouble. Over ninety-nine percent of the time, he cannot think of any.

Many of our teens have heard someone claim that the Bible is marked by contradictions and they have acquiesced, either in the name of "good science" or simply because it is their time to question authority. The wise Christian parent need not panic. After two thousand years of successfully defending itself under heavy fire, the Bible not only will withstand, but welcomes whatever questioning your teen brings to it.

True science has never been at odds with Scripture. In fact, recent scientific discoveries have proven that the Bible is an archeological document of the highest calibre. With over eight million copies sold of his book, *The Bible As History,* journalist Werner Keller writes, "These breathtaking discoveries make it necessary for us to revise our views about the Bible. Many events that previously passed for pious tales must now be judged to be historical." I could feel the author's excitement when he concluded, "In view of the overwhelming mass of scientific evidence now available, as I thought of the skeptical criticism which from the eighteenth century onward would have demolished the Bible altogether, there kept hammering in my brain this one sentence: 'The Bible is right after all!'"[8]

Not only does science support the Bible, but the writers of the New Testament were actual eyewitnesses of the life of Jesus Christ. They knew Him personally or had experienced Him in a unique way like the apostle Paul. One of the weightiest evidences for the validity of the Bible is that most of its writers suffered horrible persecution or died hideous deaths for the cause of Christ. The only explanation for their fervor that makes sense is that they had actually seen, spoken with, and shared meals with the Lord Jesus. Knowing that their lives were characterized by poverty and persecution, it is irrational to think that they would have recorded the Scriptures and then died for a lie.

Perhaps the best confirmation is the testimony of Jesus Himself. The only perfect man ever to walk our planet consistently endorsed the Scriptures as the authoritative, errorless Word of God. As Dr. Vernon Grounds wrote in *Christianity Today,* "Christ knew . . . believed . . . studied . . . expounded . . . venerated . . . respected . . . obeyed . . . and fulfilled the Scriptures."[9]

Jesus often censured the way the Bible was interpreted, but He never criticized the Bible itself. On the contrary, He who was the Word (John 1:1) based all that He said and did on the Bible. To review some of His own thoughts about Scripture, look up Matthew 5:17, 18; 22:29; John 5:39-47; 17:17.[10]

Finally, a convincing evidence of the Bible's inspiration is its unity. It is nothing less than supernatural that forty separate authors writing over a period of 1,600 years could produce a work as cohesive in both message and intent. When J.B. Phillips began work on his *New Testament in Modern English,* he did not believe the Bible to be verbally inspired (i.e., that each word was inspired or

"God-breathed").[11] But as he progressed, he became deeply impressed by the unity of the books, and declared, "In their different ways and from their different angles, these writers are all talking about the same thing and talking with a certainty as to bring a wonderful envy into a modern heart."[12]

Question #3. I have a Muslim friend in English class who asked me why Christians think they have the only true religion. So we believe in God and he believes in Allah. What's the big difference? It doesn't seem fair to try to convert him from the faith he has grown up with. Why do Christians believe that Jesus Christ is the only way to God?

If you accept the Bible as God's revelation to man, then you cannot escape the magnificent claims that Jesus made about Himself.

"I am the way and the truth and the life. No one comes to the Father except through me." (John 14:6)

"I give them eternal life and they shall never perish. . . . No one can snatch them out of my Father's hand. I and the Father are one." (John 10:28-30)

"All authority in heaven and on earth has been given to me." (Matthew 28:18)

Paul Little reminds us that "neither sincerity nor intensity of faith can create truth,"[13] and the real issue here is the question of truth. If someone tells you that the law of gravity has been repealed, and you sincerely believe it, not even the ardor of your faith will save your life should you test your mistaken belief from the roof of a tall building. As C. S. Lewis said, "Nonsense is still nonsense, no matter who believes it."

I have seldom experienced more tension in a home than the evening I observed a beautiful senior in high school arguing with her fundamentalist father over the exclusivity of Christianity. The argument had been building when she finally challenged, "But my friend is a devout Hindu, Dad. There is no way she would ever consider converting to Christianity. And why should she? How can you be so arrogant to believe that Jesus Christ is the only way to get to heaven?"

I wanted to respond to her question, to ease the strain, but I knew that it was not my place. It was obvious that this father and daughter had clashed before, now reaching an impasse. The lines had been drawn, and I sensed that the resolution of this conflict would do much to determine their future relationship. All eyes were on him.

With his lips pursed and his jaw set firmly, he finally gave in to his growing anger.

"It's just what we believe, that's all!" he shouted. "It's what we've always believed. And it's the way you were raised. You should know better!"

Embarrassed, she excused herself and ran upstairs to her bedroom. As her door slammed, I did not have high hopes for any further religious discussions she might have with her father. Neither was I surprised that upon graduation from high school, she left for the state university and stopped attending church. Her questions about the Christian faith had been sincere and obviously of great emotional value to her. Her father's failure to give them honest consideration only hastened her eventual rejection of Christianity.

As discouraging as that experience was, I recently received hope that some Christian parents are helping their teens struggle through times of doubting. Consider this letter from a teenager named Kevin:

> *Last year, on our way home from a wrestling tournament, my friend turned to me and out of the blue said, "You know, what I don't understand about Christianity is what makes it different from any other religion. What makes it right and the others wrong?"*
>
> *I was baffled and didn't know what to say to him. I stammered and stuttered and blurted out something like, "Well, it is because God said so and . . . ah . . . ah . . . you just have to believe it."*
>
> *Of course that question stayed on my mind, so I asked my father about it later. He told me, "Christianity is different because you don't have to earn your way into heaven, and because God is a loving and forgiving God. For example, Hindus live by a caste system in which some people are untouchable. And Allah did not die for the Muslim's sins—they have to earn their way to heaven."*
>
> *He continued, "Our God forgives anyone for anything, and lets the most untouchable of the untouchables enter His kingdom if they'll only believe in Him and let Him love them."*
>
> *My dad helped me so much. I understand what makes Christianity so different from other religions. Now I know what to say to someone else!*[14]

Kevin's father was wise and prepared. Out of the ten major religions of the world (Buddhism, Islam, Hindu, Confucianism, etc.), Christianity is the only one that is based upon God's grace, in that He loved us enough to send His Son to pay the price for our sins. All other religions are works-oriented, which makes the Christian faith the most wonderful news that any of our friends who are struggling to work their way to heaven could possibly hear.

Question #4. I have several friends who have no idea who Jesus Christ is. How could a loving God send them to hell?

Teens who ask this question should never be told that they are wrong. In fact, they are on the right track. God is love, and He sends no one to hell. The fact is that people who reject God's love in Christ choose hell.

In C.S. Lewis's book, *The Great Divorce*, he tells an intriguing story about a busload of people who leave hell for a brief excursion to the outskirts of heaven. Old acquaintances who now live in heaven come out to meet the passengers from hell and offer each one the opportunity to change his eternal location.

One would think that all denizens of the nether world would leap at the chance to enter heaven, but the ensuing discussions result in each passenger falling victim to his own pride and reclaiming his seat on the hell-bound bus. One of the heavenly saints observes, "There are only two kinds of people in the end: those who say to God, 'Thy will be done,' and those to whom God says, in the end, 'Thy will be done.' All that are in Hell, choose it. Without that self-choice there could be no Hell. No soul that seriously desires joy will ever miss it. Those who seek find. To those who knock it is opened."[15]

The Bible says that God is "not willing that any should perish" (II Peter 3:9, KJV). "Do I take any pleasure in the death of the wicked? declares the Sovereign Lord. Rather, am I not pleased when they turn from their ways and live?" (Ezekiel 18:23). The truth is that the door to hell is closed from the inside, and that God has done everything He can do to save us from ourselves without controverting our free will.

Because He is both a God of love and justice, He must deal with humankind's sin problem. The good news of Christianity is that God has done exactly that by sending His own Son to be crucified for our sins. He is at once both Reconciled and Reconciler! Still, there is nothing He can do for teens who choose self over God's love, and such friends will have no excuse when they stand before the judgment seat of Christ. The apostle Paul says that God has already revealed Himself to those teenagers in at least two ways:

1. God is revealed "without" through nature. Romans 1:20 testifies, "For since the creation of the world God's invisible qualities—his eternal power and divine nature—have been clearly seen, being understood from what has been made, so that men are without excuse."

Considering the information that a teen receives about God from creation alone, Paul Little believes that "we may conclude that if a man responds to the light he has and seeks God, God will give him a chance to hear the truth about Jesus Christ."[16]

2. God is revealed "within" through our conscience. Romans 1:19, NASB claims that a knowledge of God is "evident within them." Paul moves on to describe this inward knowledge by writing, "He will punish the heathen when they sin, even though they never had God's written laws, for down in their hearts they know right from wrong. God's laws are written within them; their own conscience accuses them" (Romans 2:12, 13, TLB).

"He has also set eternity in the hearts of men" (Ecclesiastes 3:11b). Therefore, we are all "without excuse."

Question #5. I have non-Christian friends who treat me better than some of the people at church. If Christianity is truth, then why are there so many hypocrites in it?

Teenagers are quick to detect duplicity in religion and are uninhibited in using it as a rationale for their own alienation from the church and their Christian parents. The National Sunday School Association asked 2,000 teens why they left the church. The youth gave "adult hypocrisy" as their second most frequent reply.[17]

My first response to youth who question the hypocrisy in the church is that they are not being severe enough. It is not just that there are some hypocrites among Christians; on the contrary, every member is a hypocrite at times, myself included. When Martin Luther said, "The face of the church is the face of a sinner," he was not criticizing Christians for their imperfection, but rather confessing to the watching world that followers of Jesus Christ are still human beings who struggle with their sin nature. I John 1:8-9a was written to Christians: "If we claim to be without sin, we deceive ourselves and the truth is not in us. If we confess our sins, he is faithful and just and will forgive us our sins. . . ."

I have noticed through the years that teenagers are attracted to a church with an active altar. When they see adults and other teens obeying God's command to "admit your faults to one another and pray for each other," they are often quick to withdraw their accusation of hypocrisy. There are few testimonies as powerful to a teen as Christians who openly confess their humanity and ask forgiveness, resolving, by God's grace, to change in the future.

I also remind teenagers that there is another way that the term "hypocrite" can be understood, as Jesus alone used it in the New Testament. He spoke of hypocrites as those who claim to know God but in reality do not. In fact, His harshest words were reserved for those who used the guise of religion to further their wickedness. His judgment on them will be incisive: "Not all who sound religious are really godly people. They may refer to me as 'Lord,' but still won't get to heaven. For the decisive question is whether they obey my Father in heaven. At the Judgment many will tell me, 'Lord, Lord, we told others about you and used your name to cast out demons and to do many other great miracles.' But I will reply, 'You have never been mine. Go away, for your deeds are evil' " (Matthew 7:21-23, TLB).

So teens have a prototype in the Lord Jesus for exposing fraud within the ranks of Christendom. "I came to bring truth to the world," Jesus said to Pilate. "All who love the truth are my followers" (John 18:37b, TLB). Instead of teens allowing their faith in Christ to be thwarted by "deceitful workmen, masquerading as apostles of Christ" (II Corinthians 11:13), they should pity such pretenders who will face the condemnation of God Himself. "Their end will be what their actions deserve" (II Corinthians 11:15b).

In the meantime, I invite teenagers to join the company of those who are not perfect, but forgiven, and who sincerely seek to follow the truth. Anyone who will help the church to maintain its integrity is not only welcome, but also much needed. Paul's words to his teenaged friend Timothy are relevant: "Don't let anyone look down on you because you are young, but set an example for the believers in speech, in life, in love, in faith and in purity. . . . Preach the Word; be prepared in season and out of season; correct, rebuke and encourage—with great patience" (I Timothy 4:12; II Timothy 4:2a).

Barry Wood has a final word of caution for youth who are considering rejecting Christianity because of the hypocrisy they observe: "You should not miss knowing Jesus because of someone else's failure. The hypocrite isn't worth missing heaven for. Don't let Satan keep you from Christ's love by filling your heart with bitterness and resentment. He'll win and you'll lose. Judging others won't spare you the judgment of God."[18]

The church at Rome received even better advice. "You, therefore, have no excuse, you who pass judgment on someone else, for at whatever point you judge the other, you are condemning yourself, because you who pass judgment do the same things" (Romans 2:1).

As teenagers critically examine their childhood beliefs, they are likely to become doubtful about many religious forms and some religious content. As their early faith no longer meets their needs emotionally, intellectually, or spiritually, they often begin to question Christianity. The wise parent realizes that their questioning does not indicate a desire to become agnostic or atheistic, but could signify their need to internalize the Christian faith and accept its beliefs as their own. That there are logical, Bible-based answers to most of their questions should encourage those parents who are willing to prepare themselves to respond.

CHAPTER
12

Satan's Great Miscalculation
The Evangelistic Effect of Confronting the Enemy

All religions are coming around to Satanism. We're in the very throes of a new Satanic Age.
—ANTON LAVEY, AUTHOR OF *THE SATANIC BIBLE*

I have given you authority over all the power of the enemy.—JESUS

A PERSONAL ENCOUNTER WITH the occult proved to be the seventh leading cause for teenagers in this study to choose for the Lord Jesus Christ. Initially I was surprised to find so many teens citing a reaction against satanic influence as their entry level into Christianity. Then I began a careful investigation of the escalation of teen involvement with the occult.

After almost two years of gathering data on this phenomenon, I am no longer as astounded by nor as skeptical of observations like this one from Peter Micha, pastor and occult researcher: "It is a fact that, through heavy metal music, fantasy role-playing games like Dungeons & Dragons, slasher movies, etc., between seventy to seventy-five percent of today's teens have dabbled in the occult— and thirty percent of those actually become involved in the occult world."[1]

THE DEVIL MADE ME DO IT

Their attorneys described Pete Roland, James Hardy, and Ron Clements as "good, clean-cut young men," not unlike "most typical high school students." But on December 6, 1987, with their unsuspecting friend, Steven Newberry, they drove to a secluded patch of woods outside Carl Junction, Missouri. After sacrificing a cat to pay homage to the devil, the three teens turned on Newberry, chanting, "Sacrifice for Satan!"

Newberry's panicked attempt to escape was futile. Armed with baseball bats, they pommeled their friend. Approximately seventy blows later, young Newberry lay dead. With the sacrifice of their comrade completed, Roland testified that he expected Satan to appear and grant each of them great power. Instead, they received life sentences in prison with no possibility for parole.

When the jury inspected a box with their prized possessions in it, they found "a satanic notebook with demonic doodlings, a carved skull with a nail driven through it, and diabolical-looking rock posters and album covers."[2] One attorney stated that the boys' favorite song was Megadeth's "Black Friday," which gloated, "My hammer's a cold piece of blood lethal steel, I grin while you writhe in the pain that I deal."[3]

A few years ago, an incident as macabre as Newberry's murder would have been dismissed as a social anomaly, an aberration that did not merit the public's attention or alarm. The luxury of such disregard can no longer be afforded, according to Maury Terry, author of *The Ultimate Evil*. "There is compelling evidence of the existence of a nationwide network of satanic cults, some branched into child pornography and violent sadomasochistic crime, including murder. I am concerned that the toll of innocent victims will steadily mount unless law enforcement officials recognize the threat and face it."[4]

Many Christian authorities on the occult agree with Terry. "There is a frightening increase of devil worship among American teenagers," reports Bob Sussman, author of *America's Best Kept Secret*. "Over the last few years, there has been a tremendous increase of police reports on this subject in every state of the nation. Some experts claim that it is going on in every community in our country. In one of the most advanced civilized countries in all of history, Satanism is alive and rampant."[5]

Headlines from across the nation attest to the rise of Satanism among teenagers. Houston, Texas: "Devil Worship: Troubled Teens See Outlet for Rebellion." Chicago, Illinois: "Teenaged Satanists Vandalize Church." Norfolk, Virginia: "Satanist, 16, Prime Suspect in Ritualistic Murder." Los Angeles, California: "Teen Satan Worshippers: Police Confront a Modern Nightmare."[6]

It is becoming increasingly more difficult to dispute the data being gathered by researchers. From the extensive number of preschool cases of the satanic ritual abuse of children, it is certain that "a massive indoctrination of school children into Satanism is going on."[6] We do not have good cause anymore to doubt Arthur Lyons, who writes in his book, *The Second Coming: Satanism in America*, "The United States harbors the fastest growing and most highly organized body of Satanists in the world."[7]

THE SEQUENCE OF SATANIC SEDUCTION

Because adolescence is a period when most people experiment with their belief systems, many teenagers are particularly vulnerable to the mystique and perceived power the occult offers. Until recently, satanic activities have been viewed as fantasy fare for horror movies and the bizarre novels of Stephen King. But now, occult investigators and public officials are unanimously warning good parents that the occult is a viable presence in their children's lives and no teen is immune from involvement in it. A fairly typical pattern for teen entanglement in Satanism has emerged.

The teenager will most likely begin as a "dabbler," or one who takes a superficial interest in the occult. "These ritual dabblers are usually middle-and upper-class teens of high intelligence," says Detective Robert J. Simandl, a specialist in ritual abuse for the Chicago Police Department. He adds, "They are generally creative, curious, and possibly underachievers with low self-esteem."[8]

There are many reasons that youth might become involved in Satanism. Mike Warnke, author of *The Satan Seller*, claims that the Enemy uses the same three techniques to tempt teens as he used to tempt the Lord Jesus in the wilderness: gratification of the ego, gratification of the flesh, and power.[9]

Dale Trahan, program consultant with Hartgrove Hospital in Chicago, believes that teens lured into the occult share two basic characteristics. First, the youth sense that they are "different" from others; that they do not fit in with their "straight" peers. Even though they might be popular, they feel that they do not belong with the regular crowd. Second, they are disturbed by a future over which they have no power. They feel that they are at the mercy of fate and are not in control of their destiny.[10]

Other lures into Satanism include the use of the occult to

demonstrate opposition to authority, the imitation of their favorite heavy metal heroes who promote satanic themes (like Ozzy Osbourne, AC/DC, Megadeth, Slayer, Black Sabbath, Venom, Iron Maiden, and Motley Crue), and a dissatisfaction with traditional religion. In fact, teens who disengage from the church are especially susceptible to the occult. Having been reared on a belief in the supernatural, the transition is easy and appears reasonable for them to leave the pious trappings and boredom of organized religion for the excitement and power offered by Satanism. Often feeling that they do not belong in the mainstream, these teens begin to look for ways to meet their needs, alternatives to their current lifestyle.

When youth have reached this point, the occult has no need to brainwash them. The seductive promise of power is too appealing for them to resist. They truly believe that they can get what they want by involvement in the occult. Such teens then explore these new ideas through literature and films found in libraries and video stores. Their changing perspective on life is now characterized by an acceptance of their being different from others ("Nobody really understands me"), a growing sense of superiority ("I have a power that none of my friends have"), and a brooding cynicism about those in authority ("They are all wrong—the church, society, my parents—and I am right"). Armed with this destructive attitude, they begin to seek out like-minded peers.

Once they are involved with a group, the next step of the seduction is initiated, pulling them deeper within the occult. The trap is usually set at a party where free drugs and sex are readily available. As the night progresses, the teen is photographed in some compromising situation. The cult members use the photo to black-mail the teen into signing a pact with the devil. This contract guarantees that the new member will sacrifice himself to Satan at a specified age to demonstrate the ultimate gift to his new master.[11]

Fourteen-year-old Tommy Sullivan, raised in a devout Christian home, signed such a contract with the devil shortly before he committed suicide. His pact read, "To the greatest of demons: I would like to make a solemn exchange with you. If you will give me the most extreme of all magical powers, I will promise to commit suicide. I will tempt teenagers on earth to have sex, have incest, do drugs, and worship you. I believe that evil will once again rise and conquer the love of God."[12]

Young Tommy, whose interest in the occult began when his public school teacher assigned her students to prepare a report on Satanism, crossed the line from being a dabbler in the occult to becoming a deluded collaborator with evil.

SATAN'S GREAT MISCALCULATION

Even though the effects of the satanic movement among American teenagers can be harmful and sometimes even lethal, one of the remarkable finds of this study is that many modern-day teens are compelled toward Christianity because of their negative experience with the occult.

The word occult means "hidden" or "concealed." Historically, Satan's most productive strategy has been to deal in secret, camouflaged and undetected as he "shoots from the shadows" (Psalm 11:2). It has been his practice for centuries to divide and despoil from a distance, always encouraging Christians to fight one another instead of turning their attention and spiritual weaponry against him. Indeed, until recently, mainline Christianity has effectively ignored the existence of the Enemy, and her paltry gains in evangelism are the result. But with the documented rise of Satanism in America, theologians and church members alike are beginning to take seriously the reality of objective evil in the personal forms of the Devil and his emissaries.

The machinations of Satan are no longer restricted to the darkness. This change of tactics is most likely prompted by his awareness that we are living in the last days, and his time is short. He has decided to go public with both his forces and philosophies, and in so doing, has declared open war on American teens via black metal music, demonic movies and literature, and peer-induced satanic activities. In my judgment, the Devil has made a great miscalculation. He should have left American teenagers to themselves. After interviewing scores of teens who became Christians only after realizing the existence of and truth about Satan, my advice to his infernal majesty would have been to have remained hidden. His exposure has always been his downfall.

Scripture supports this observation. During his ministry in Asia, the apostle Paul openly confronted the forces of darkness. Immediately after the exposure of satanic activity in Ephesus, Scripture records, "When this became known to the Jews and Greeks living in

Ephesus, they were all seized with fear, and the name of the Lord Jesus was held in high honor. Many of those who believed now came and openly confessed their evil deeds. A number who had practiced sorcery brought their scrolls together and burned them publicly. . . . In this way the word of the Lord spread widely and grew in power" (Acts 19:17-20).

The open unmasking of Satan inspired widespread evangelism among those involved in the occult in the province of Asia. If the following responses of the youth in this survey are any indication, I predict a similar revival among teenagers today—precisely because the Enemy has overreached himself again.

My dad led me to the Lord in my grandparents' living room when I was five years old. But I didn't really become a Christian until two years ago when I had a run-in with Satan's forces. I was watching the movie A Nightmare on Elm Street *when I suddenly realized that Satan was real. That's when I knew whose side I wanted to be on. It's amazing how God used Satan's tool to change my life!—*BARRY, 16

*I saw a "Geraldo" special about Satanism on TV and it literally scared the h— out of me. The devil worshippers on the show were weird and pretty frightening, but I thought the Christians were pretty cool. One of them reminded me of a friend of mine at school. He's the one who told me how I could be a Christian too.—*JIM, 15

*I gave my life to Jesus Christ the morning after my best friend and I were playing with a Ouija board at her house. We weren't taking it very seriously—asking the board whether or not we would get married, and what his name would be. It did freak us out a little bit when it seemed like the board was actually giving us answers. But we just decided to blow the whole thing off. That night, when we went to bed, we both could hear heavy breathing, and we were convinced that something evil was in the room with us. I really prayed for the first time since I was a little kid. The next morning, we went right to the youth pastor at our church, who explained to us what was going on and how we could be safe from it. That's the day that both Sandy and I became Christians.—*JILL, 16

When people ask me if I've read This Present Darkness, *I tell them, "I don't have to; I've already lived it." I knew that demons were real from the time I was about four years old. My father was an alcoholic, so one minute he could be nice and the next he would get really violent. Maybe because I was young, God gave me special insight to see that it wasn't just the liquor that drove him on when he physically abused me and my mother. I could actually see and feel that someone else, someone very evil was inside him. That's probably why I always forgave him for what he did to me, and I know it's why I learned to pray for God's protection.*

—PATRICIA, 14

Testimonies like these convince me that God can turn Satan's own strategies against Him to effectively evangelize teenagers. There are many things that a concerned Christian parent can do to join God in this battle for the souls of America's youth.

What's a Parent to Do?

1. Exchange your skepticism for a biblically informed commitment to imitate the Lord Jesus' attitude regarding the enemy.

"Jesus said to [the Devil], 'Away from me, Satan!' " (Matthew 4:10).

"Adults often don't have a willingness to acknowledge the occult," claims Officer Jeorge Fierro of the Allegan County Sheriff's Department in New Mexico. He adds, "Parents say, 'It couldn't happen here,' or they simply choose not to recognize it. Others try to ignore its presence, hoping that Satanism will just go away."[13]

Historically, ignoring the existence of Satan has been one of Christendom's more grievous blunders. Widely respected British theologian David Watson states, "The 'enlightened' churches of today, which do not believe in the existence of the Devil, are so often lifeless and powerless. They are truly under his power but fail to realize it."[14]

The pages of the New Testament are burgeoning with the ubiquitous conflict between the Lord Jesus and the powers of darkness. If He was not commanding the demon hordes to release their hold on the pitiful possessed, then He was directly confronting Satan himself and teaching His disciples to do the same. One can be certain that His heavenly jihad directed against the "god of this world" never left His consciousness.

His relentless mission became even clearer the night He was betrayed and handed over to His enemies for crucifixion. He stood alone in the Garden of Gethsemane and announced, "Now is the time for judgment on this world; now the prince of this world will be driven out" (John 12:31).

The Church must never forget that "the reason the Son of God appeared was to destroy the devil's work" (I John 3:8). Furthermore, Paul exhorts us "to keep Satan from gaining the advantage over us; for we are not unaware of his schemes" (II Corinthians 2:11).

To be ignorant of Satan and his ways is to give him added leverage over us and enervate the mission of the Church. Christian parents must become aware of his devices and be able to recognize his malevolent presence in the world. McNeile Dixon once wrote, "The kindhearted humanitarians of the nineteenth century decided to improve on Christianity. The thought of Hell offended their sensitivities. They closed it, and to their surprise the gates of Heaven closed also, with a melancholy bang. The malignant countenance of Satan disturbed them. They dispensed with him and at the same time, God took His departure."[15]

2. Understand the goal of and philosophy behind Satanism.

"Wisdom is supreme; therefore get wisdom. Though it cost all you have, get understanding" (Proverbs 4:7).

In his book, *Michelle Remembers*, psychologist Lawrence Pasner warns parents that Satanism is not secretive about its major objective: complete domination of the souls of the coming generation. "One of its primary aims," Pasner asserts, "is to destroy the belief system within a teenager, to make that youth turn against what he believes in—especially in terms of who God is, and to desecrate all manner of church institutions to which a teen could be attached."[16]

The goal of Satanism has never changed. It is the thorough destruction of the temporal and eternal lives of those teenagers involved. It is the complete reverse of Christianity, its moral system insisting that good is evil, and evil is good. Satanism represents the glorification of carnal pleasure. From the Satanic Bible comes its major tenet: " 'Do what thou wilt' shall be the whole of the Law."

Satanism intentionally perverts and inverts everything good, discrediting God and glorifying the Devil. For example, the redemptive blood of Jesus Christ (symbolized in the communion service) is mocked by teens in satanic cults by drinking the blood of human or animal sacrifices. Communion bread, symbolic of Christ's sacrificial body, is routinely mixed with blood, urine, semen, or feces, and then eaten by devil-worshipping teenagers. Often the bread is replaced by human flesh itself.

The cross, signifying salvation among Christians, is used upside down by satanists as a denouncement of God's love. Captain Brian Young of the Iowa State Police reported that one young man who was experimenting with the occult turned every cross in his parents' home upside down in order to curse his family. No one even noticed the act until after the confused teenager committed suicide.

Brian Sussman adds that Satanists also believe there is power or energy within humans and animals. This power can be absorbed by the Satanists through rituals ranging from sexual activity to murder, dismemberment, or even cannibalism. The Satanist's logic (revealing one of the major reasons they target teenagers for involvement) is that the more helpless or younger the victim, the more innocent; the more innocent, the more precious to God; the more precious to God, the greater the defilement; thus the more power for the Satanist to acquire. Children and teens are believed to have great energy within them.[17] For Satan, there is no trophy more priceless than a young teenager.

3. Learn to recognize the behavioral red flags of satanic involvement.

"Have nothing to do with the fruitless deeds of darkness, but rather expose them" (Ephesians 5:11).

The teen most vulnerable to the lure of Satanism, is usually characterized as one having low self-esteem, physically awkward, not fitting into a peer group at school, alienated, isolated, no sense of humor, sexually confused, bored, and artistic.

There are danger signs for parents who are concerned about youth who might be involved with or susceptible to Satanism. A teen may be connected to the occult if he or she:

- is suicidal or has attempted suicide
- holds undue fascination with death, torture or suicide
- alienates himself from family and/or religion
- shows violent and/or aggressive behavior directed toward parents, siblings or authority figures
- reveals evidence of self-mutilation (boys on the wrists and

155

forearms; girls on the wrists and breasts) and/or tattooing
- abuses drugs or alcohol
- experiences a drastic change in grades
- has high truancy from school
- has a compulsive interest in occult materials, fantasy role-playing games, music, films and videos all with the themes of death, suicide and torture
- possesses a "Book of Shadows," usually an innocent-looking spiral notebook with heavy metal groups and satanic symbols on the outside

On the inside, such a book contains poems about death, suicide notes, and the planned date of the teen's suicide to complete his contract with Satan. Elgin State Police Trooper Jim Vargus, a noted authority on cult practices, claims that the book will be written in code, possibly the Viking or witch's alphabet. He suggests that other items to search for are various ceremonial knives, bones and religious trappings such as robes, candles and chalices.[18]

The following are a number of satanic symbols of which Christian parents should be aware.

The PENTAGRAM is the most powerful satanic symbol, used when Satanists seek to contact evil spirits or desire to be possessed by a demon or Satan. The bottom point represents the spirit of man which is pointed down (toward hell). The other points represent earth, fire, wind, and water.

The CROSS OF NERO was named after a Roman emperor infamous for persecuting Christians. Characterized by an inverted, broken cross, it has evolved from being a peace symbol to its present status among occult groups as a symbol of the defeat of Jesus Christ.

The "MARK OF THE BEAST" or Satan is used as general symbol of satanic involvement.

The FERTILITY CROSS or ANKH, originally an Egyptian symbol for life and sexual reproduction, is used for satanic rituals involving sex.

The SYMBOL OF ANARCHY represents the rejection of all law, discipline and rules; a popular symbol of heavy metal rock fans.

The CROSS OF CONFUSION is another Roman symbol; it usually signifies a challenge to the verity of the Christian faith.

The BLOOD RITUAL SYMBOL represents human and animal sacrifices; often found at ritual sites.

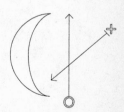

The BROKEN CROSS or SWASTIKA is a mystic symbol of the Old World adopted by the satanic elements of the Nazi party as their emblem and a symbol of anti-semitism.

The EVIL EYE or "ALL-SEEING EYE OF SATAN" represents Satan's watch-fulness and is often used in a cursing ritual; the tear signifies Satan's sorrow that all men are not under his control.

4. Do not hesitate to seek professional help.

"Listen to advice and accept instruction, and in the end you will be wise" (Proverbs 19:20).

There is no shame in admitting the need for securing support outside the home. No family with teens in America is free from crises. "Admit your faults to one another," directed James the apostle, "so that you may be healed" (James 5:16). The church is not an elitist gathering of parents with no problems, but a hospice for those who have the courage to face them. Besides the pastor of your local congregation, other intervention sources for teens who might be involved in the occult are as close as your telephone.

- •Warnke Ministries (Information and counseling for occult involvement) 1(800) 345-0045
- •Teen in Trouble? 1(800) 442-HOPE
- •Dr. Dale Trahan Hartgrove Hospital, Chicago (Information and treatment programs for teens involved in Satanism) 1(312) 722-3113
- •Cult Awareness Network 1(312) 528-4401, P.O. Box 381, Crystal Lake, Illinois 60014. This volunteer organization is dedicated to "bringing to the public awareness of the harmful effects of destructive cults and providing information and support for families, as well as assistance to former followers in their re-entry into society."

5. Formulate your own battle plan against the enemy.

"Put on the full armor of God so that you can take your stand against the devil's schemes" (Ephesians 6:11).

Scripture says that "the whole world is under the control of the evil one" (I John 5:19). Evangelizing teenagers then is, in essence, reclaiming them from the grasp that the world has on them. Such an effort will not be without danger or difficulty. But the wise parent will enter this worthy battle with several factors in mind.

- The victory is already yours in Christ Jesus. In John 11, Jesus thanked the Father for answering His prayer even before Lazarus was raised from the dead. In the same way, we can be confident that our success over Satan has already been won—no matter what the circumstances may presently appear. "Death has been swallowed up in victory . . . thanks be to God! He gives us the victory through our Lord Jesus Christ" (I Corinthians 15:54-57).

- Your most effective weapon against the enemy is the Word of God. David Watson believes that the battle against Satan "requires a detailed knowledge of the Bible, committed to memory so that it is readily available for taking immediate offensive action. Every verse of God's Word that you have 'hid in your heart' is a potential sword thrust to put the devil to flight."[19] Just as the Lord Jesus engaged Satan in the wilderness with Scripture, so we parents are to fill our arsenal with God's Word. When battling the enemy for the allegiance of a teenager, I always find strength in verses like these.

"Greater is he that is within you, than he that is in the world."
(I John 4:4, KJV)

"Resist the devil, and he will flee from you." (James 4:7)

"I have given you authority . . . to overcome all the power of the enemy." (Luke 10:19)

"The God of peace will soon crush Satan under your feet."
(Romans 16:20)

"And the devil . . . was thrown into the lake of burning sulfur, where the beast and the false prophet had been thrown. They will be tormented day and night for ever and ever."
(Revelation 20:10)

- Remember that your success in battle comes from your position in Christ. You must never confront the Enemy on your own. In Acts 19, the seven sons of Sceva, all non-Christians, confronted a single demon without the authority of Jesus.

  "The evil spirit jumped on them and overpowered them all. He gave them such a beating that they ran out of the house naked and bleeding" (Acts 19:16).

  No man outside of Christ has the wherewithal to assault Satan's strongholds. "Apart from me you can do nothing," said Jesus (John 15:5).

  " 'Not by might nor by power, but by my Spirit,' says the Lord Almighty" (Zechariah 4:6).

  For the believer whose authority over Satan emanates from the shed blood of the Lord Jesus Christ, then God is "a strong tower against the foe" (Psalm 61:3). Such a parent will have "divine power to demolish strongholds" (II Corinthians 10:4) and will learn that "not even the gates of hell will prevail" against them (Matthew 16:18).

No teenager is beyond God's ability to rescue.

CHAPTER
13

Parents Are Still the Answer

For love is stronger than death. . . . Many waters cannot quench it.—SOLOMON

My TEENAGE DAUGHTER WAS for sale last year. Did I love her? Of course! Did I like her? Of course not! I wasn't sure exactly where to place the ad, but the "Help Wanted" section seemed most appropriate. Anyone who is exhausted from daily exposure to the "terrible twos" will come to understand, after one week of living under the same roof with a highly volatile, hormonally charged adolescent female, the wisdom behind the adage, "Small kids, small problems; big kids, big problems!" I remember when our biggest problem was trying to find a thumb-sucking detox center.

Fortunately, there were no takers for my ad. Just when I was about to join F.A.D.D. (Fathers Against Difficult Daughters), my independent descendant left for a visit with a Christian friend of hers in Tennessee. The thoughtful girl who returned to us was nothing like the one who just a few weeks earlier had announced that she hated the whole family and couldn't wait to go to college.

If I hadn't been so pleased by the transformation, I'd have responded, "Okay, kid, who are you? And what have you done with my daughter?" Instead I meekly queried, "So, did you enjoy yourself, honey?"

"Oh, Dad!" she burst forth. "It was just too cool! We went

horseback riding and shopping and I met the neatest Christians!"

After a complete debriefing, I realized what had happened. My daughter had experienced an "attitude transplant" during a series of Bible studies with her friend in Nashville. Although she had grown up in a Christian home and attended church from infancy, she had reached that crucial stage of making the Christian faith her own. She had been one of the ninety-five percent of American teens who need an "inner conversion" experience with the Lord Jesus.

I suppose I had for years considered her to be a Christian, mainly because she made a profession of faith at an early age, was baptized into the church, and lived in our Christian family. And yet I knew that sometime during adolescence she would have to face the questions, "What do I really believe?" and "Am I going to live my adult life as a Christian?" That I believed she was a Christian was insignificant compared to the fact that now she believes she is one.

Her decision to follow Christ and internalize Christian values made an immediate impact on our home. Before the transformation, conversation with this high school sophomore—when she decided to grace us with her presence—consisted of three grunts and a rolling of the eyes. The house was viewed merely as a pit stop, a place to grab a snack, change an outfit, and borrow some money. Who is this strange "new creature" (II Corinthians 5:17) who let one of her sisters borrow a sweater yesterday and helped another one fix her hair for church this morning? I may not recognize her, but I'm not complaining.

My wife and I are firm believers in the evangelism of teenagers. It can certainly change the atmosphere of a home.

TEENAGERS MAKE WONDERFUL CHRISTIANS

Teens make wonderful Christians because they sparkle and snap with energy. They are perpetual motion machines, euphoric one moment and despondent the next—but never boring. It can exhaust you just to watch their restlessness, but you can feed off it, too. In fact, the parent as evangelist can capitalize on the enthusiasm of youth. Their commitment to a person, an idea, or a cause may appear transient, but it will be all-consuming. In more ways than just those mentioned in this book, the wise parent will gently channel this energy in the direction of Jesus Christ.

Teenagers make remarkable Christians because of their sense of humor. They love to make fun of the self-inflicted solemnity of adults. They puncture our pomposity with their quick wit, and are jokingly irreverent about adults, relations, government, their friends, and often even themselves. Youth have a marvelously silly streak, and if we parents just loosen up a bit, we would find ourselves growing closer to our teens while we laugh together over some innocent foolishness of theirs. I am also convinced that if we could dispense with our compulsive concern about good taste, take ourselves less seriously, and cultivate our own sense of humor, we could more effectively evangelize our teens.

Teens make wonderful Christians because they are honest and spontaneous. While questioning everything, they lead us to re-examine our own assumptions and beliefs. Someone once said that "teenagers don't cause problems in the home; they reveal them." Their relentless pursuit of truth inspires and disturbs me at the same time, but I know it is vital to my own growth as a Christian. We really should not think so highly of ourselves. The truth is that while we are praying for and evangelizing our teenagers, they are most certainly discipling us. God uses their candor about religion to shock us out of our spiritual rut and bring us back to authentic Christianity.

Resiliency is a strong characteristic of teens, fortunately, and most of us parents can rely on it. God created them this way for at least two important reasons. First, it helps them bounce back after they have made mistakes, assuring us that there is always hope they can be reached for Christ. Second, it gives parents second and third chances when we fail them. If we try one method of discipline or guidance that doesn't work, they give us another chance. It is difficult to ruin a resilient teen and inflict irreparable scars on them. Teenagers make good forgivers.

PARENTS ARE STILL THE ANSWER

And so we come full circle. In Chapter 1 we learned that the top fear among non-Christian parents is that their teens might become involved with drugs, while the worst fear of Christian parents is that their children might decide against Christianity. It is only fitting, then, that the survey this book is based upon revealed that Christian parents are the key to evangelizing their own teenagers. The number one predictor of teenage faith is parental influence.

The teens in this study cited seven factors (church, friends, youth pastor, crises, media, questions answered, and encountering Satan) as the immediate reasons they chose to become Christians. These seven evangelistic entry levels are far more effective if the parents are simultaneously doing "affirmation evangelism" with those teens. Researchers agree that the values of Christian parents exert the most important influence on their teenagers' values. Most studies reveal clear parallels between the children's faith and the faith of their parents.

We have discussed many means by which we can ensure the transmission of our Christian faith to our beloved teenagers. For most of these strategies to work, parents are still the answer. By way of summary, if parents will focus on four basic areas, the evangelism of their teens will be under way.

1. Christian parents must lead by example.

How is this generation, so suspicious of manipulation, so wary of hypocrisy, to be convinced that Jesus is Lord? There is only one way: they must see Him in us. If we are to pass on the faith to our children, then we must model authentic Christianity. It is not enough merely to be religious or moral. If we are to incarnate the message of Christ for our teens, then we must stand for the same things for which Jesus stood. Jesus championed the helpless, confronted the corrupt, loved His enemies, and eventually died for His commitment to the truth.

Teens have always been attracted to the Cross. They thrive on great causes against impossible odds, and when they observe their parents dying to self and living for others, Christianity begins to look like a cause worthy of their commitment. When youth see their parents refusing to capitulate to the egocentrism of secular society and actively fighting injustice because the love of Christ compels them to do so, they are constrained to consider Christianity for themselves.

Teenagers discover truth via relationships, and parents who desire to evangelize them will focus on the same. The main trouble of youth is not with Christ's admonition to love their neighbor, but with the more abstract concept of loving a distant God. Worship, a sense of what is sacred, a mystical hunger for prayer—these come harder for the young than concern for their neighbor. Of the two dimensions constituting religion—the vertical (loving God) and the horizontal (loving their neighbor)—they gravitate toward the horizontal.

It is difficult for teens to relate to God in the same way their parents think of Him. The "otherness" of the vertical dimension gives them a problem. And I don't think God minds one bit. In fact, one reason that teens are so reachable for Christianity is that, being extremely relational, they are already close to the heart of God. The Lord could have used many teens I know to write the book of I John. They love its two-fisted charge to make certain that our belief impacts how we treat others. "For anyone who does not love his brother, whom he has seen, cannot love God, whom he has not seen. . . . Whoever loves God must also love his brother" (I John 4:20, 21).

One teenage friend of mine wrote a beautiful account of his belief. "God is to me the Person who gives my life meaning. I could never accept the idea of a God separate and far away, because I know that God really is love—a love that transcends all human differences and binds all people who love Him in union. I also know that the God I speak of is the God of Christianity, because in Jesus Christ, I see the everyday reality of that love."

The Christian parent is someone who believes not in a set of truths but in a person—Jesus Christ. That is what the Christian faith is, and it will never be easy to pass on. There is no infallible formula to follow. But one condition *sine qua non* is that parents possess it themselves. It means living in such a way that our lives would be unexplainable if God did not exist.

2. Christian parents must trust their teenagers.

The best way to show teens that you love them is to communicate your sincere trust in them. The Bible says that "if you love someone, you will be loyal to him no matter what the cost. You will always believe in him, always expect the best of him, and always stand your ground in defending him" (I Corinthians 13:7, TLB). Adults will more effectively evangelize the next generation by treating them like adults.

Of course there are risks involved in giving freedom to teenagers. Parents are painfully aware of the damage teens can do to themselves if they are given indiscriminate liberty. But overprotectiveness and smothering solicitousness are tendencies against which youth have always had to protect themselves from well-intentioned parents. The fact is that the apprehensive, controlling Christian parent is the very one who, more often than not, drives the teenager away from the faith.

Parents who are hopeful and trusting are much better evangelists than those who are perpetually suspicious and doubting. Research shows that teens feel closer to parents who create an atmosphere of trust and acceptance, of hopefulness and flexibility. Such parents know that inherent dangers come with trust, but they accept them because they realize that New Testament evangelism is historically a "high-risk/high-reward" phenomenon. Though teens can wound themselves on freedom, their imminent salvation makes the risk worthwhile.

There is, of course, a sense in which teens should earn your trust and be given every opportunity to do so. But many youth have become trustworthy as a direct result of being trusted by their parent even when those teens didn't believe in themselves. The wise parent seeks the balance between earned and unmerited trust, never forgetting that the teen who can be trusted is more likely to be the one who eventually trusts in Christ.

3. Christian parents must learn to take the spiritual pressure off their teenagers.

No one can be forced into Christian commitment. By its very nature, religious commitment is a decision that can only be made willingly, free from manipulation or coercion.

That you thrive on 5:30 a.m. devotions does not mandate that your teen must be a spiritual giant before breakfast. Just because you have chosen full-time ministry as a vocation, your children should not be badgered into following suit and belittled if they do not. You regret your choice not to go to the mission field, but it is as unfair as it is unproductive to expect your child to go in your place.

Parents who persist in keeping on the pressure should not be surprised to find their teens eventually rejecting the faith. Many teens feel that spiritually coercive parents really do not love them for who they are.

Recently a college freshman who was struggling with her faith confided in me, "I know that my mother is worried about me, but I am so sick of her preaching. She phones me under other pretenses, but I'm always waiting for the sermon that she'll slip in somehow. She cannot talk to me as a person; she's always got to bring God into the conversation. She might think that she loves me, but I'm getting the message that she'll only truly love me when I'm the good little Christian girl that she wants me to be."

PARENTS ARE STILL THE ANSWER

Dr. David Elkind, author of *All Grown Up and No Place to Go*, reminds us that, when confronted by spiritual pressure from parents, younger children blame themselves for not measuring up to standards. Elementary school children will usually blame the world for their duress. But adolescents blame their parents.

The wisest course for Christian parents is to stop worrying about their teens and trust them to the Lord's care. Worry is not only irrelevant and irresponsible, it is irreverent. Anxiety over the spiritual welfare of our children, as accepted and widespread as it is in the church, still precludes God's ability to bring them to faith. When I finally decided to follow God's advice, "Don't worry about anything; instead pray about everything" (Philippians 4:6a, TLB), the spiritual attitudes of all the teens in our home improved dramatically.

4. Christian parents must learn how to love and be loved.

I was not raised in a Christian home, so it is no surprise that my father and I were never close—a fact that has caused me a lot of guilt and occasionally crippled my spiritual growth. Not having experienced the type of love I felt I needed as a teen, predictably I have struggled with receiving love from my heavenly Father.

Those who get to know me recognize early on that it is far easier for me to give than receive, a personal trait that has plagued me for years and made it difficult to establish close friendships. The sense of low self-worth I inherited as a teen followed me into my adult years and marked each relationship with the same lack of intimacy I'd had with my father. I would let friends get only so close before I would withdraw, convinced that the more they knew me, the less they would like me. One day, out of frustration, a pastor friend bravely exhorted me, "Bob, I think I finally understand you. You desperately need to be loved, and the irony is that you won't really let anyone love you. My guess is that your biggest problem is that you won't let God love you! Every relationship you have would improve if you could get this fixed."

His words cut me to the quick, and I knew that he was right. There had been times when even the intimacy I had with my own children had been bittersweet, a reminder of what I'd missed as a child. Still, I had little confidence that I could change. This friend encouraged me in my devotional life to focus on Scriptures that spoke of God's love for me. I sincerely wanted to experience wonderful passages like Ephesians 3:17-19: "And I pray that you, being rooted and established in love, may have power, together with all the saints, to grasp how wide and long and high and deep is the love of Christ, and to know this love that surpasses knowledge."

But not until last Christmas did the Holy Spirit bring the kind of healing I needed to realize the fullness of God's love. We had invited my parents to spend the holidays with us, and as usual, I had mixed emotions. I loved my father, but the distance that marked our relationship during my teen years had only gotten worse as I approached middle age.

I felt that he had always been my critic, austere and disapproving, and I was seldom comfortable around him. I had convinced myself that he did not love me, and even if he did, it never crossed my mind to try to understand why he was unable to express it. Never mind that he was raised as an orphan in a non-Christian home and had ample reasons for not being able to articulate his love to his children. I was determined to hold onto my self-pity and sense of regret.

It is a common complaint among teenagers that their parents insist on treating them like children and refuse to recognize their maturation. During my parents' visit at Christmastime, I learned that the reverse can also be true: many parents could justly complain that their children have categorized them and dismissed the possibility that they can change. I had long ago resolved not to look for love from my father.

Although we both became Christians after I left home, we frequently argued over personal beliefs. Eventually we began to avoid each other, and I felt we had a tacit agreement to steer clear of anything resembling a serious talk. But during his holiday visit, my father broke that contract. . . and I know my life will forever be changed.

I was about to join the family for our annual viewing of *It's a Wonderful Life* when I noticed Dad sitting alone at our dining room table reading his Bible.

"Hey, Dad, the movie's about to start. Let's go downstairs."

He looked up and replied, "Listen, son. I can't do that. We need to have a talk first."

At that moment, I was no longer a forty-three-year-old Bible professor with three teens of his own. I was a boy of fourteen who had just been summoned by his father for a lecture.

But this man, whom I realize now I hardly knew, looked me directly in the eyes and related a simple story. His words were measured, but charged with emotion.

"When I was at Mayo Clinic this summer, I realized there was a chance I might not survive the surgery I was facing. My attending physician was a Christian and asked me one day why I seemed troubled. I told him that if I died, my only regret would be that, although I became a Christian late in life and have had a wonderful ministry, my own son dislikes me."

As he spoke, I sensed that these thoughts were even more difficult for him to express than they were for me to hear. And so I quietly listened, forcing myself to meet his eyes.

"My doctor and I talked for awhile, and then he advised, 'Mr. Laurent, I think you offended your son while you were raising him, and you need to ask his forgiveness.' "

Realizing what he was about to do, I remember thinking, *I'm not ready for this! How am I supposed to react?*

Dad rose from his chair and stepped toward me. "Son, I know now that I hurt you deeply through the years, and though I don't deserve it, can you find it in your heart to forgive me?"

I will never be able to describe the emotions I was feeling just then. But one thing I knew for certain: he was a brave man, and I was proud of him for taking this risk. Still, I was too stunned to speak, so he filled the silence.

"There's one other thing I've been wanting to tell you, son, but I never knew how." With a quivering voice, he said, "I love you, Bob."

My tears were instantaneous. The embrace that followed will always be a prized memory for me. Months later, I am still experiencing the spiritual exhilaration and healing that resulted from our reconciliation.

Simon Peter was right when God inspired him to write, "Love each other deeply, because love covers over a multitude of sins" (I Peter 4:8).

Love is the key for reaching your children. Christian parents who have close friendships with their teens make the ultimate evangelists. And the good news is that as the parent of a teenager, you can save the precious years that my father and I tragically wasted. Your love for your teens will lead them to Christ, and through Him, they will not only find life, but also a parent who is their best friend.

ENDNOTES

Chapter One

1. Richard Wilkerson, "Changing the Lives of Youth in America," *Evangelizing Youth,* ed. Glenn C. Smith, (Wheaton, Illinois: Tyndale House Publishers, Inc., 1985): 11.
2. Jay Kesler, "Bringing Youth to Christ," *Evangelizing Youth,* ed. Smith, (Wheaton: Tyndale House, 1985): 55.

Chapter Two

1. Ron Hutchcraft, "Evangelizing Today's Youth," *Evangelizing Youth,* ed. Smith, (Wheaton: Tyndale, 1985): 105.
2. Charles G. Morris, *Psychology: An Introduction,* Englewood Cliffs, New Jersey: Prentice Hall, 1988), 387.
3. Jay Kesler, "Bringing Youth to Christ," *Evangelizing Youth,* ed. Smith, (Wheaton: Tyndale, 1985): 56.
4. Roy G. Irving and Roy B. Zuck, *Youth and the Church,* (Chicago: Moody Press, 1968), 14.
5. Kesler, "Bringing Youth to Christ," 50.
6. William R. Bright, "How You Can Tell Others About Christ," *Evangelizing Youth,* ed. Smith, (Wheaton: Tyndale, 1985): 85.
7. David A. Roozen, "Church Dropouts: Changing Patterns of Disengagement and Re-entry," *Review of Religious Research* 21, No. 4 (Fall 1980): 427.
8. H. N. Malony, "Conversion," *Psychology and Religion,* ed. David G. Benner, (Grand Rapids, Michigan: Baker Book House, 1988): 20.
9. Ibid., 19.
10. Erik Erikson, *Adolescence: Identity and Crisis,* (New York: Doubleday, 1968), 172.
11. G. Stanley Hall, *Adolescence,* (New York: McGraw-Hill Book Company, 1904), 214.
12. Dennis Miller, "Christian Teenagers: They're Leaving the Flock," *Moody Monthly,* September 1982.

Chapter Three

1. Craig W. LeCroy, "Parent-Adolescent Intimacy," *Adolescence,* 1988, 137.
2. Jim Petersen, *Evangelism As a Lifestyle,* (Colorado Springs: Navpress, 1980), 25.
3. Gail Sheehy, *Passages,* (New York: Bantam Press, 1976), 48, 49.

4. Paul Borthwick, But You Don't Understand, (Nashville: Thomas Nelson Publishers), 1986, 76.
5. Ibid., 77, 78.
6. Robert Munsch, *Love You Forever*, (Willowdale, Ontario: Firefly Books, 1986).
7. Taylor Caldwell, *Great Lion of God*, (Garden City, New York: Doubleday, 1970), 453.
8. Myron Brenton, *How to Survive Your Child's Rebellious Teens*. (New York: Lippincott, 1979), 50.

Chapter Four
1. Joyce Vedral, *My Teenager Is Driving Me Crazy*, (New York: Ballantine Books, 1989), 8.
2. Elizabeth Winship, *Reaching Your Teenager*, (New York: Houghton Publishing, 1983), 42.
3. Merton Strommen, "Five Cries of Youth," *Ladies Home Journal*, (March 1985), 29.
4. Vedral, 130.
5. Robert Coles, quoted by R. Goleman, *The New York Times*, (April 14, 1989), 47.
6. Vedral, 135.
7. Ann Epstein, quoted by R. Goleman, *The New York Times*, (April 14, 1989), 47.
8. H. Samm Coombs, *Teenage Survival Manual*, (Lagunitas, California: Discovery Books, Inc., 1989), 73.
9. Merton Strommen, *Five Cries of Parents*, (New York: Harper & Row, 1978), 33.
10. Peter Walker and Herbert Thompson, *Natural Parenting*, (New York: Interlink, 1987), 84.
11. Craig W. LeCroy, "Parent-Adolescent Intimacy," *Adolescence*, (1988), 139.
12. Ibid., 139
13. Ibid., 139
14. Ibid., 139
15. Paul Borthwick, *But You Don't Understand*, 80, 81.
16. James Dobson, *Focus on the Family*, (January 1988), 4.
17. Steven Kelman, "These Are Three of the Alienated," in *New York Times Magazine*, (Oct. 22, 1987): 39.
18. Roger Paine, *We Never Had Any Trouble Before*, (New York: Stein & Day Publishers, 1975), 52.
19. James Dobson, *Focus on the Family*, (May 1988): 12.

20. Jim Petersen, *Evangelism for Our Generation*, (Colorado Springs: Navpress, 1985), 33.

Chapter Five
1. Quoted in *U.S. News and World Report*, 30 June 1986.
2. Quoted in *The New York Times*, 12 March, 1987.
3. Terrance D. Olson, *Ebony*, (21 March , 1988): 31.
4. Garrison Keiller, *Lake Wobegon Days*, quoted in *U.S. Catholic*, (January 1987), 6.
5. Jim Petersen, *Evangelism As a Lifestyle*, 107.

Chapter Six
1. Search Institute, *Source*, Vol. V, No. 4, (December 1989).
2. John Conger, *Adolescence and Youth*, (New York: Harper & Row, 1977, 536.
3. Dennis Miller, quoted in *Evangelizing Youth*, ed. Smith, (Wheaton: Tyndale House, 1985), 313.
4. Stuart Briscoe, *Where Was the Church When the Youth Exploded?* (Grand Rapids: Zondervan Publishing, 1972), 9-11.
5. Princeton Religion Research Center and The Gallup Organization,*The Unchurched American*, (Princeton, New Jersey: 1987), 27.
6. George Gallup, quoted in *Evangelizing Youth*, 312.
7. *The Unchurched American*, 8.
8. James Kolar, quoted in *Evangelizing Youth*, 205, 206.
9. Ibid., 106, 107.
10. George Gallup, quoted in *The Elkhart Truth*, 19 May, 1990.
11. Karl Menninger, *Whatever Became of Sin?* (New York: Hawthorn Books, Inc., 1973), 228.
12. George Gallup, quoted in *Evangelizing Youth*, 312.
13. Lincoln Research Center, *Adolescent Disengagement from the Church*, 1986, 42.

Chapter Seven
1. James DiGiacomo and Edward Wakin, *We Were Never Their Age*, (New York: Holt, Rinehart and Winston, Inc., 1972), 174, 175.
2. Jim Petersen, *Evangelism As a Lifestyle*, (Colorado Springs: Navpress, 1980), 34.
3. Joe Aldrich, "Developing Vision for Disciplemaking," in Jim Petersen, *Evangelism for Our Generation*, Colorado Springs: Navpress, 1985, 77.
4. *USA Today*, 21 June 1990, 4.
5. Petersen, *Evangelism for Our Generation*, 39.

6. Ibid., 107.
7. Dann Spader, "Tired of Band-Aid Approaches to Youth Work?" *Moody Monthly,* (January 1984), 55.
8. Myron Brenton, *How to Survive Your Child's Rebellious Teens,* 140.
9. Joyce Vedral, *My Teenager Is Driving Me Crazy,* 83.
10. Fred Hartley, *Dare to Be Different,* (Old Tappan, New Jersey: Fleming H. Revell Company, 1980), 37.
11. Paul Borthwick, *But You Don't Understand,* 47.

Chapter Eight
1. Ben Misjuskovic, "Loneliness and Adolescent Alcoholism," *Adolescence,* Vol. XXIII, No. 91, (San Diego: Libra Publishers, Inc., Fall 1988): 508.
2. Jim Elliott, handout at Semp '90, Moody Bible Institute Summer Evangelism Encounter.
3. "Students Today: Money-Motivated," *USA Today,* May 1988.
4. Christopher Lasch, quoted by Jim Petersen, *Evangelism for Our Generation,* 20.
5. Lawrence Kutner, *The New York Times,* 3 March 1988.
6. Howard. Burbach, "An Empirical Study of Powerlessness Among Teenagers," *The High School Journal,* April 1972, 343.
7. George Hunter, *The Contagious Congregation,* Nashville: Abingdon Press, 1980, 51.
8. Peter Marshall, *Disciple,* (New York: McGraw-Hill, 1963), 74.
9. Dan Morris, "Does Anyone Care About Our Teens?" *U.S. Catholic,* (Jan. 1985): 31.
10. Dennis Miller, quoted in *Evangelizing Youth,* 313.
11. Ibid., 251.
12. Dann Spader, quoted in *Evangelizing Youth,* 313.

Chapter Nine
1. Renee Stovsky, "How to Handle Stress," *Daily Courier-News,* 30 September 1990.
2. Diane Eble, "Too Young to Die," *Christianity Today,* (20 March, 1987), 20.
3. Ibid.
4. Fern M. Eckman, "Teen Suicide," *McCall's,* (October 1987), 71, 72.
5. Diane Eble, "Too Young to Die," 21.
6. Ibid., 24.
7. Lawrence Kerns, "How to Tell If Your Teen Is Suicidal," *Elgin*

Courier News, 7 March 1989.

8. Eble, 23.
9. June Toellner, "An Answer to Teenage Suicide: 'Soul Searching' ," *Chicago Tribune,* 3 May 1987, 47.
10. Elwood McQuaid, "Divorce," *Moody Monthly,* (February 1987): 33.
11. Dann Spader, quoted in *Evangelizing Youth,* 315.

Chapter Ten
1. Paul King, "The Hidden Persuaders: Sex, Drugs, and Advertising," WGN presentation, 4 January , 1991.
2. Ibid.
3. Bob DeMoss, *Citizen,* Vol. 4, No. 8, (20 August , 1990).
4. Dennis Miller, quoted in *Evangelizing Youth,* 247.
5. Dave Hart, *Media Update,* Vol. 8, issue 3, 2.
6. Bob DeMoss, *Citizen,* 2.
7. Dave Hart, *Media Update,* 2.
8. Bob DeMoss, 2.
9. Dave Hart, 3.
10. Laurence Steinberg, "Adolescence: A Growth Period Conducive to Alienation," *Adolescence,* (Winter 1987): Vol. 22, No. 88, 131, 133.
11. DeMoss, 3.
12. Tom Alesia, "What Gives With Video Violence?," *Elgin Daily Courier News,* 5 April 1990.
13. Ibid.
14. Ibid.
15. *Daily Courier News,* Editorial, May 1990.
16. *Daily Courier News,* "Programs Come and Go, But Violence Is Constant," 30 January 1990.
17. Franky Schaeffer, *A Time for Anger: The Myth of Neutrality,* (Westchester, Illinois: Crossway Books, 1982), 15.
18. Paddy Chayefsky, *Network,* (Pocket Books Publishing, New York: 1976), 76.
19. David Seamonds, quoted in *Standing In The Gap,* ed. John Youngberg, (Berrien Springs, Michigan: Marriage and Family Seminars, 1986): 53.
20. Richard Fredericks, "Television and the Christian Family," (Ph. D. project for the course, "Seminar in Religious Education Curriculum," Andrews University, 1981).

Chapter Eleven

1. Jean Piaget, *The Development of Thought,* (New York: The Viking Press, 1975), 23.
2. Richard Havighurst, *Adolescent Character and Personality,* (New York: Wiley Publishers, 1955), 10.
3. David Baldwin, quoted by Holly Green in "Are You Raising A Spiritual Drop-Out?" *Today's Christian Woman,* (May-June 1990), 50.
4. Sandy Larsen, "Listening to Our Children That They Might Believe," *Christianity Today,* (29 May 1981): 15.
5. Ibid.
6. Lawrence O. Richards, "The Hardest Test at School: When Your Teen's Values Are Challenged," *Parents & Teenagers,* 634, ed. Jay Kesler, (Wheaton, Illinois: Victor Books, 1984).
7. Jacques Ellul, *Money and Power,* (New York: Seabury Press, 1969), 123.
8. Werner Keller, *The Bible As History,* (New York: William Morrow and Company, 1956), 3, 5.
9. Vernon G. Grounds, "Building on the Bible," *Christianity Today,* (November 25, 1966): 28.
10. Fritz Ridenour, *So What's the Difference?,* (Glendale, California: Regal Books, 1975), 22.
11. Ibid., 23.
12. J. B. Phillips, *Letters to Young Churches,* (New York: Macmillan Publishing Company, Inc., 1947), 12.
13. Paul Little, *How To Give Away Your Faith,* (Downer's Grove, Illinois: Inter-Varsity Press, 1966), 70.
14. Kevin Anderson, "I Learned the Difference," *Campus Life,* (January 1990), 12.
15. C. S. Lewis, *The Great Divorce,* (New York: Macmillan Publishing, Company, Inc., 1946), 72, 73.
16. Paul Little, *How To Give Away Your Faith,* 69.
17. T. R. Torkelson, "Sick of Hypocrisy," *Signs of the Times,* (Berrien Springs, Michigan: March 1970), 3, 4.
18. Barry Wood, *Questions Non-Christians Ask Today,* (Power Books, Old Tappan, New Jersey: Fleming H. Revell Co., 1986), 52.

Chapter Twelve

1. Bob Sussman, "America's Best Kept Secret: A Look at Modern-day Satanism," video documentary, 1990.
2. Bob Larson, *Satanism: The Seduction of America's Youth,* New York: Thomas Nelson Publishers, 1989, 103.

3. Ibid.
4. Maury Terry, *The Ultimate Evil*, Garden City, New York: Doubleday and Company, Inc., 1987, 511.
5. Bob Sussman, *America's Best Kept Secret*.
6. Ibid.
7. Arthur Lyons, *The Second Coming: Satanism in America*
8. Deborah J. Mayberry, "The Seduction of Satanism," *Notes 'N News*, Vol. II, Issue 10, October 1990, 16.
9. Mike Warnke, *The Satan Seller*, 144
10. Deborah Mayberry, "The Seduction of Satanism," 16.
11. Ibid.
12. Bob Larson, *Satanism*, 103.
13. Dale Dieleman, "Danger of the Occult Is Real," *The Grand Rapids Press*, 14 October 1990, 1.
14. David Watson, *Hidden Warfare: Conquering in the Spiritual Conflict*, (Kent, England: STL Books, 1972), 72.
15. McNeile Dixon, quoted by F. J. Rae in "The Expository Times," Vol. lxvi, 215.
16. Bob Sussman, *America's Best Kept Secret*.
17. Ibid.
18. Deborah Mayberry, 17.
19. David Watson, *Hidden Warfare*, 113.